"This is a fantastic book. It offers a timely, refreshing and insightful antidote to the popular, highly sanitized, mainstream accounts of what organizational culture is and how it works. It is written in a rigorous, incisive and humorous way. In this regard, rather than seeing Collins as purely being an academic, it is better to also at least figuratively think of him as part public intellectual, part surgeon, and part stand-up comedian."

Prof. Cliff Oswick, of City University, London

Rethinking Organizational Culture

What is organizational culture? Why does it matter? This book demonstrates that conventional wisdom on this fundamental business topic has surpassed its usefulness. The author wants neither to praise scholarship on culture nor to bury it – rather he wants to build something fit for purpose by reflecting on the power of stories and storytelling.

Rethinking Organizational Culture argues that the entrenched models of organizational culture wrench thinking, feeling, and action from a context that intuition warns us are complex and problematic. Arguing that novels and novelists offer an opportunity to redeem 'organizational culture', the text invites readers to recognize that stories of organization offer connections with organizational profanity, organized polyphony, and the organizationally prosaic.

A stimulating and provocative read, this book will be welcomed by students, scholars, and reflective practitioners across the business field.

David Collins is Professor of Management at Northumbria University, UK, and Visiting Professor in Management at the University of the Faroe Islands. His previous books include *Organizational Change, Management Fads and Buzzwords, Narrating the Management Guru, Stories for Management Success, Management Gurus,* and *The Organizational Storytelling Workbook.*

Routledge Focus on Business and Management

The fields of business and management have grown exponentially as areas of research and education. This growth presents challenges for readers trying to keep up with the latest important insights. *Routledge Focus on Business and Management* presents small books on big topics and how they intersect with the world of business research.

Individually, each title in the series provides coverage of a key academic topic, whilst collectively, the series forms a comprehensive collection across the business disciplines.

Innovation Research in Technology and Engineering Management
A Philosophical Approach
Marc J. de Vries

Rethinking Organizational Culture
Redeeming Culture through Stories
David Collins

Management in the Non-Profit Sector
A Necessary Balance between Values, Responsibility and Accountability
Renato Civitillo

Fearless Leadership
Managing Fear, Leading with Courage and Strengthening Authenticity
Morten Novrup Henriksen and Thomas Lundby

Clusters, Digital Transformation and Regional Development in Germany
Marta Götz

For more information about this series, please visit: www.routledge.com/ Routledge-Focus-on-Business-and-Management/book-series/FBM

Rethinking Organizational Culture

Redeeming Culture through Stories

David Collins

Made in Kilmarnock

Routledge
Taylor & Francis Group

LONDON AND NEW YORK

First published 2021
by Routledge
2 Park Square, Milton Park, Abingdon, Oxon OX14 4RN

and by Routledge
605 Third Avenue, New York, NY 10158

Routledge is an imprint of the Taylor & Francis Group, an informa business

British Library Cataloguing-in-Publication Data
A catalogue record for this book is available from the British Library

Library of Congress Cataloging-in-Publication Data
Names: Collins, David, 1966– author.
Title: Rethinking organizational culture: redeeming culture through
    stories/David Collins.
Description: Milton Park, Abingdon, Oxon; New York, NY:
    Routledge, 2021. | Includes bibliographical references and index.
Identifiers: LCCN 2020056429 (print) | LCCN 2020056430
    (ebook) | ISBN 9781032004891 (hardback) | ISBN
    9781003174431 (ebook)
Subjects: LCSH: Organizational change—Social aspects. |
    Corporate culture. | Organizational behavior. | Organizational
    sociology.
Classification: LCC HD58.8 .C6423 2021 (print) | LCC HD58.8
    (ebook) | DDC 302.3/5—dc23
LC record available at https://lccn.loc.gov/2020056429
LC ebook record available at https://lccn.loc.gov/2020056430

ISBN: 978-1-032-00489-1 (hbk)
ISBN: 978-1-032-01760-0 (pbk)
ISBN: 978-1-003-17443-1 (ebk)

Typeset in Times New Roman
by Apex CoVantage, LLC

Contents

Figures

1 Introduction

Rethinking organizational culture

We are now so familiar with the suggestion that organizational problems and organizational processes may be constituted usefully in cultural terms that it is easy to forget that this is, in fact, a novel development. This little book understands that 'culture' represents a comparatively recent introduction to the discourse of management and yet it has been designed to intervene within this discourse so that we may now rethink organizational culture. To secure this end, the book will offer critical reflections upon the ways in which a concern with 'culture' has informed a) our understanding of the nature of social organization and b) our appreciation of the essence of managerial work. This book will, therefore, consider the manner in which an understanding of 'culture' entered and altered the field of management. It will also probe the ways in which 'culture' informs our appreciation of managing.

Yet, even as we share these reflections, we will suggest that the discussion of 'culture' (or, if you prefer, the active consideration of the manner in which social norms, beliefs, and values shape conduct within work organizations) too often acts to deform our understanding of the problems of working and the processes of managing.

Building cultures for business success

Atkinson's (1997) attempt to build the cultures necessary for business success offers – unknowingly – a very useful illustration of the manner in which culture informs and in so doing deforms our understanding of social processes. Writing in the late 1990s, but building upon, what we might term, an end-of-the-century motif, Atkinson asserts that: 'Culture change is *the* critical "business issue" for organisations as we enter the next century' (8 emphasis in original).

Atkinson's preferred rhetoric is, of course, designed to establish a) the centrality of 'culture' and b) the consequent need to manage cultural change in order to meet the imputed challenges of the new millennium. In pursuit of these twin goals, he invites his readers to 'Imagine what your business could become if you knew you couldn't fail in implementing a strong and healthy culture' (8). Yet, even as he reaffirms the position that 'Culture is the most important aspect of a business' (17), Atkinson introduces a range of supplementary assertions which suggest that 'culture' really merits much more careful reflection.

Atkinson begins with the assurance that culture is 'the fabric of the business' (16). In the absence of a more detailed definition of 'culture', which might account for the warp and weft of this 'fabric', Atkinson, however, assumes that it is sufficient to state, simply and blandly, a) that culture involves 'Values' (16) and b) that these are sufficiently important to merit capitalization.

Not all values (capitalized or otherwise), however, are, it seems, useful to organizations:

> A positive vibrant culture will ensure that staff expend their energy in the interests of the business because the culture will reflect the accepted way of managing or leading. More negative cultures will create a climate where staff are driven to do things because they fear the consequences of "not doing so". Some companies have interesting cultures where nothing in particular is valued or communicated – people just do the job. You can imagine that the results are less than awe-inspiring.
>
> (Atkinson, 1997, 16)

Plainly, Atkinson (1997: 16) has a very fertile imagination because in the light of these reflections, he invites yet another flight of fancy and in so doing suggests additional questions designed, it appears, to help 'organizations' to construct the positive values and the 'vibrant' cultures that he prizes. This is, we should note, a fairly lengthy list of increasingly trite and tiresome questions. I will offer only a sample:

> Imagine being able to shape and design a 'corporate culture' the way an architect designs a house. What would you do first? How would you set empowering Values which would inspire others to perform within set standards? How many Values would you work on and how would these relate to the goals of business

I too have questions; so, so many questions.

• Why are 'Values' capitalized but 'empowerment' (for example) appears only in lowercase?

- Are values really discrete entities that we may lift, transport and (re)arrange? Are values (capitalized or otherwise) usefully considered to be just like piles of bricks?
- And if we can, indeed, build values, can we do this *sui generis*? Or are there limits – associated for example with history, with community, with context – to the changes that may be wrought in the name of 'business interests'? For example can we, as Atkinson seems to suggest, simply pick and choose among these building blocks; demolishing some 'Values' and reassembling others to reflect our plans and our whims?
- And crucially we might ask: What is actually meant by 'Values' and how do these relate to culture?

Atkinson (1997: 143) avoids this issue for a very long time. Eventually, however, he does provide a response to this, the last and perhaps the most pressing of my questions. He tells us that:

> 'A culture is the set of values, behaviours and norms which tell people what to do, how to do it and what is acceptable and unacceptable'.

Yet, this (late) statement on the essential nature of culture cannot disguise Atkinson's continuing confusion about the manner in which the social world coalesces. At the outset, for example Atkinson (1997: 8) suggests that culture is an organizational attribute. Culture is, he tells us, '*the* critical "business issue"'. And yet within just a few pages, Atkinson shifts his ground such that culture becomes, not an attribute but the essence of organization, 'the fabric of the business' (16). Later, however, a new and altogether more mechanistic account of 'culture' is offered. Thus culture is, as we have seen, (also) to be recognized as an array of organizational/business 'building blocks' (126) formed, apparently, from 'Values' (16).

So . . . it appears that Atkinson's strategies for success require us to accept that organizations 'are' cultures and yet 'have' cultures. And if that were not sufficiently confusing, it seems that we must also accept that an organization's cultural attributes are just like *Lego* bricks insofar as these may be built and demolished endlessly to reflect the desires of management actors.

Managing culture is, of course, generally acknowledged to be a tricky undertaking, yet it would appear that in Atkinson's hands 'culture' is altogether more mercurial than *anyone* imagined!

*****

Atkinson, I suspect, would regard my intervention, my mocking interrogation of his imaginings as, in any sense, impertinent: he prefers action

to reflection. Moreover, he suggests that these facets of life may be separated. And having secured this separation to his own satisfaction, Atkinson
chooses to pursue the 'how' rather than the 'why' (18) of culture change.
Yet, any attempt to separate action and reflection, both doing and thinking
about it are intensely problematic. Indeed, we would do well to note that
Atkinson's disavowal of reflection and his attempt to privilege practical
action over theoretical (you may choose your own epithet – for the moment
I'll go with) navel-gazing is, of course, a position rooted very firmly 'in
theory'. Thus, to suggest that theory and action are separate and to suggest
that reflection may be subordinated to action are, of course, to project a
theoretical appreciation of the world – albeit one that few sensible commentators would actually support (see Collins, 1998, 2018).

*****

I have enjoyed picking at the surface of Atkinson's cultural schema.
Yet, my comments are not simply mischievous. There is some mischief,
of course, but my observations do have a serious intent; they have been
designed to demonstrate:

- That there is, at the heart of the culture change discourse, confusion as
  to the essential nature of organizational culture.
- That this confusion is largely ignored, or brushed aside, by so many of
  those accounts of culture that have been prepared for students and for
  'executives'.

This confusion relates:

- firstly to the conceptualization of culture,
- secondly to the tendency to view culture through a lens ground by the
  imputed 'needs' of business
- thirdly to the willingness to adopt a perspective that views culture only
  from the top-down; and
- fourthly to the assumption that culture controls and programmes our
  thoughts and actions.

Conceptualizing culture

Despite initial hesitations and a false start, it is clear that Atkinson does eventually settle on a preferred account of the nature of organizational culture.
Culture, he suggests, is to be regarded as 'a thing' – an organizational attribute. For Atkinson, therefore, culture is however vaguely understood, something that organizations 'have'. Yet, this position is disputed (at some level

by Atkinson himself and) by alternative perspectives which suggest that culture is more usefully conceptualized as the essence of social organization – something that the organization 'is' (see Ackroyd and Crowdy, 1990; Martin, 1992). The fact that Atkinson ignores this issue suggests that he has no real grasp on the debates that shape this arena. But ignorance is bliss, since in choosing to ignore the debate as to the very essence of culture, Atkinson is empowered to assume that the cultural form, which he deems necessary for the new millennium, is a) under his control and will b) bend to accommodate his whims and his preferred strategies of management.

To answer a question, posed earlier (if somewhat rhetorically), Atkinson does, in fact, tend to assume that 'culture' exists *sui generis;* it is for Atkinson *a thing* untrammelled by history and context. 'Culture' is it seems his to change.

Business needs

Atkinson (1997) asserts the presence of 'the interests of the business' (17) and assumes that these will act to unify both cultural values and organizational conduct. This assertion of common business interests, we should note, is useful for Atkinson's purpose. Indeed, we would do well to note that this support for the unifying nature of 'business interests' allows Atkinson to construct a curious, contradictory and self-serving world. For Atkinson, therefore, organizations are, simultaneously, harmonious and yet prone to disruption. But we need not worry about this contradiction because 'culture' (or if we are honest, changes to culture planned and managed by leaders on behalf of 'the organization') will sweep away the disruptive conduct that so troubles Atkinson.

The assumption that conflict is a temporary disruption to the natural order of 'the organization', which cultural change will, nonetheless, resolve is, of course, rhetorically powerful: It enables, for example, the casual disparagement of plurality. Yet, if we accept that conflict is, at least, an organizational possibility, then Atkinson's commitment to a monolithic account of 'the organization' and its cultural attributes is both, curious and ultimately impractical. Thus we should note that in refusing to negotiate with those who might choose to see the world and its problems differently, Atkinson's approach surely prevents the realization of any useful tactic whereby commitment to change, by agreement, might be fostered!

Perhaps this is why 'empowerment' is rendered only in lower case.

A top-down view

Atkinson suggests, as we have seen, that cultures may be understood from a vantage point that is defined by 'the interests of the business'. While refusing to offer any proof that might justify such a bold projection, Atkinson simply asserts that business organizations *have* cultures, while adding that, too often, these cultural formations fail to support business.

These delinquent formations include 'old cultures' that are 'not exactly geared up' for [Total Quality Management] (121) and 'traditional cultures' which exhibit a litany of failings that, for the author, seem scarcely to need rehearsal but would include 'poor layout and design of office and manufacturing areas, dirty and uncared-for staff facilities, poor lighting and environmental conditions, etc.' (121).[1]

To these, apparently hide-bound and outmoded, cultural forms, Atkinson adds 'weak' cultures, 'unhealthy' cultures and 'fear/ blame' cultures, which apparently contrast poorly with 'strong', 'positive' and 'vibrant' cultures. Yet if the 'organization' is naturally harmonious and unified by 'business interests', how can we account for a cultural formation that is shaped by fear?

Furthermore, we might ask:

- Are there agreed indicators of 'strength', 'weakness' and 'vibrancy' in this context?
- His fertile imagination aside, what gives Atkinson the right to decide, from the top-down, which formations are 'weak', which are 'strong' and which exhibit vibrancy?

Or perhaps less rhetorically: The suggestion that those cultures which are inclined to question the over-arching, top-down claims of 'the management' are, in truth, 'weak' simply fails to understand organizational plurality; organization viewed from the bottom-up. We might inquire therefore: Is a workplace where union representatives seek consultation on work design and on matters related to health and safety (to offer but two examples) really weak, negative, moribund? I don't think so!

I suggest that an organization that *really* listens to, takes note and acts upon the concerns of its employees *especially where these relate to health and safety matters* is one that deserves to be known as 'strong', 'vibrant' and/ or 'healthy'.

Culture as collective mental programming

Having assumed that culture is an organizational attribute that is a) known only to the organizational apex and b) under the control of leading executives, Atkinson (1997: 143) feels empowered to assert that culture, vaguely built upon and derived from 'Values', actually dictates our conduct. Thus, Atkinson asserts that 'culture' tells us 'what to do' and 'how to do it'. But, if this is the case, how can we explain those choices that depart from the apparent prescriptions and proscriptions of cultural life?

Collins (1998: 119) offers a response. He advises that culture seldom operates with the majesty as suggested by Atkinson. Looking back on his own conduct and on the conduct of those around him, this little deviant signals his willingness to work within and around what Atkinson would surely assume are the non-negotiable *diktats* of (Scottish) culture and society:

> In each of our own lives we can all, I am sure, find instances of . . . cultural renegotiation and modification. For example we might 'fiddle' our expenses, or 'fiddle' an insurance claim perhaps because the company is 'fair game'. We may, in spite of legal and religious prohibitions, and in spite of the frowns of our elders, argue that fiddling the company is acceptable because this form of individual action against a large company is not regarded as being 'real' theft in our eyes. Equally we may choose to procure resources from our place of employment (pens, stamps, a desk, a computer) based upon a similar understanding that such actions should not really be considered as theft. However, and in spite of such acts of theft, we probably regard ourselves as up-right, law abiding and, culturally speaking, mainstream.

Scott (1987) takes this account of plurality a step further *without resorting either to autobiography or thievery*. Thus, Scott suggests that actors may choose to give voice to culturally rooted declarations which they know to be bogus! Commenting, for example, upon the relationship between Rwanda's Tutsi and Hutu peoples, Scott (1987: 50–51, original emphasis) observes that the pastoralist Tutsi, who were the feudal lords over the agriculturalist Hutu, pretended publicly that they lived entirely on fluids; the milk and blood products taken from their herds. This narrative, the Tutsi believed, made them appear more awesome and disciplined in the eyes of the Hutu. And yet despite such claims, Scott observes that the Tutsi did, in fact, rather enjoy meat and ate it surreptitiously:

> Whenever their Hutu retainers caught them *in flagrante delicto* they were said to have sworn them to secrecy. One would be astonished if, in their own quarters, the Hutu did not take great delight in ridiculing the dietary hypocrisy of their Tutsi overlords. On the other hand, it is significant that, at the time, the Hutu would not have ventured a public declaration of Tutsi meat-eating and the public transcript [that is the official, public, version of the truth] could proceed *as if* the Tutsi lived by fluids alone.
>
> (50–51)

In your own life I am sure that you can find similar instances when you (or others around you) have voiced (cultural) ideas and sentiments, which, even if they are not quite bogus, are nonetheless rather a long way from the truth. For example my experience suggests, that when new or prospective clients visit your workplace, you and your colleagues will 'put on a show'; you will, if my experience is any guide, set aside your differences to suggest a relationship other than that which generally prevails on a day-to-day basis.

Martin (1992: 3) offers an account of culture which addresses many of the concerns raised in our discussion of Atkinson's work and provides, in addition, insights that we will later use to advance our critique of those models that, for students of management, purport to explain organizational culture. Martin's summary of 'culture', as we shall see in a moment, is significant because it highlights the significance of plurality and history. Indeed, her account of culture advises that those who would intervene to change culture should take care to acknowledge and, having done so, should take time to explore the manner in which forms of thinking and patterns of speaking become crystallized as cultural norms. Crucially, and quite unlike Atkinson, Martin reminds us that these cultural norms may reflect privilege and, we should note, may entrench prejudice. Nonetheless, Martin is clear that cultural norms will be open to (re)interpretation and, as we shall see, remain vulnerable to subversion:

> As individuals come into contact with organizations, they come into contact with dress norms, stories people tell about what goes on, the organization's formal rules and procedures, its informal codes of behaviour, rituals, tasks, pay systems, jargon, and jokes only understood by insiders and so on. These elements are some of the manifestations of organizational culture. When cultural members interpret the meanings of these manifestations, their perceptions, memories, beliefs, experiences, and values will vary, so interpretations will differ – even of the same phenomenon. The patterns of configurations of these interpretations, and the ways they are enacted, constitute, culture.
>
> (3)

*****

Despite Martin's insights and indeed our own intuitions as regards the nature and complexity of our organized lives, it would be fair to say that the analyses of 'organizational culture' that have been prepared for students, managerial leaders, and policy-makers, more generally, are seldom properly embedded within an account of historical matters, which reflects and respects the inherent social dynamics of organization. Yet, we must also acknowledge that the protestation that *culture needs history and context* may not take us very far unless we are willing to reflect critically upon our own reading of 'history'.

McCrone (1993) captures this point rather well. Discussing Scottish culture, he suggests that Scots history is very much like Scotland's topography. He tells us that there are a few peaks that, because they are prominent in the mind, tend to shape identity for the Scots. These peaks might include the *Battle of Bannockburn, the Declaration of Arbroath,* and *Culloden;* yet for the most part, Scottish history is, so to speak, down in the glens and shrouded in mist. Or as Sellar and Yeatman ([1930] 1938: viii) put it:

> History is not what you thought. *It is what you can remember*
> (viii, original emphasis)

Yet even this classic, if comic, statement merits qualification: History is not simply what you can remember it is, instead, what we care to recall.

The peaks of English (whig) history (see Butterfield, [1931] 1973), for example, might include *Magna Carta, Mafeking, the Great Exhibition,* and *the Battle of Britain.* Less prominent in the mind, I suggest, would be the incidents at *Peterloo* and *Orgreave Colliery.* Indeed, few English, I suspect, would understand that for some highland Scots, 'the union flag',[2] to this day, represents an artefact of colonial oppression, known locally as 'the butcher's apron'!

Boris Johnson, perhaps the dimmest man ever taken to be clever, demonstrates, what we might term, a trained ignorance of history. Indeed, he (like Atkinson) appears to possess a solid tin ear when it comes to matters of difference. Rebuking those who would pause to reconsider Britain's colonial and imperial histories, its conquests, its massacres, its gunboat diplomacy, its role in the trade that saw 12 million enslaved Africans trafficked across the Atlantic as chattels, Boris Johnson, Britain's Prime Minister, has warned the nation's public service broadcaster (the BBC) that it is time to stop the 'self-recrimination and general wetness' (*The Independent*, 25/08/2020). So I ask:

- What might it mean to be 'wet'? And are we really content to allow those with tin ears to lecture us on history and difference?
- Is it *really* 'wet' to reflect upon Britain's role in the slave trade?
- What might this assertion of 'wetness' say to the descendants of slaves and to those Britons who would know of their own complex and painful family histories?
- Is it 'wet' for me as a Scot to wonder about a 'national anthem' – apparently *my* national anthem – which devotes a verse to the need to crush my restive countrymen?

• Is it 'wet' (generally or otherwise) to suggest that we might now rethink, review, and re-evaluate the models of 'culture' (and by implication, context and history) that we teach our students and which we share with 'executives'?

*****

But it is not only historical myopia which limits our appreciation of 'culture'. There is, too, a process of *Bowdlerization* present within accounts of organizational culture and cultural management, which tends to limit (and to censor) the manner in which thought, speech, and action at work are represented.

Culture and Bowdlerization

Since at least the time of the Hawthorne Studies, scholars of management have understood that work is important economically *and* socially (Wright, 1994). Many of us, after, all meet our sexual partners through 'work'. Indeed, many individuals form and develop relationships at work that cause subsequent marital breakdown. Yet accounts of organizational culture – especially those focused upon the articulation of tools and techniques designed to secure culture change – ignore this important aspect of social life, reducing us all to the status of joyless, sexless drones.

When I read texts on 'culture' and 'change' prepared for students and for 'executives', I am struck by the absence of 'non-work' (see Sims, Fineman and Gabriel, 1993). Thanks to a combination of my own experience and the advice offered by my elders (many of whom volunteered for duty in World War II), I know that there is a fine art to skiving, shirking, and malingering. I also understand that such actions, while contrary to the teachings of those who would 'change our cultures', often represent thoroughly sensible and rational choices! Moreover, through some combination of experience and more formal education, I also understand that many forms of theft are socially organized, justified, and maintained (Mars, 1982). Yet, when I read textbooks on culture and change there is, in effect, no real analysis of the social world wherein such values are developed and maintained. Within texts prepared to educate current and future practitioners of management on the social organization of the workplace, no one steals. I would add, too, that in such texts no one skives, no one shirks, no one malingers, and no one laughs. Or I should say that no one laughs in that explosive, profane fashion that is truly infectious. Moreover, we should note that no one flirts. No one is ever angry, violent, envious, drunk, or dishonest. And no one ever curses.

I mean, can we take, seriously, texts which promise to unlock thought and to reprogramme action and yet exclude the single word, now so commonly employed that it is, for many Britons, a form of punctuation?

I ask you: what use is a text based, ostensibly, around the consideration of thoughts, feelings, speech and action at work where no one *fucking* swears?

*****

And with swearing on my mind . . .

This morning from within the COVID-19 pandemic, a very polite and educated friend voiced a complaint which is, I believe, instructive on key questions which *should* arise whenever we speak of culture and change:

'Why don't politicians resign when they screw up; when they side with their chums to screw us over or when they just lie?'

Demonstrating the role which swearing may perform as a form of punctuation, my friend then added a statement on cultural values which suggests a dynamic appreciation of civic society:

They used to *fucking* resign!
And for a damn sight less than anything these *fucking* jokers have done!'

Of course, we do have a tendency to romanticize our past. History is, as we have seen, that which we choose to recall. So it is probably worth conceding that I am pretty sure that not all politicians 'in the past' considered their position in the light of 'scandals' and, having done so, chose to resign and quietly to withdraw from public life. But I think my friend is broadly correct. It seems to me that British politicians did, once upon a time, take responsibility for policy delivery and would resign when they breached public expectations of competence and probity. That British politicians now fail to do this is, of course, plainly lamentable. Yet this civic tragedy is nonetheless illuminating for our purposes because the willingness to lie, obfuscate, and obscure the truth of the situation by offering 'alternative facts' demonstrates, I suggest, a certain cultural dynamism that is lost on those who have made a business of 'culture change'.

The fact that politicians and their advisors now fail to resign, as my friend puts it 'when they *fuck* up; *fuck* us over or, simply, when they are caught *fucking* lying' demonstrates, I suggest, that the manners and mores that shape conduct within Whitehall have changed *and within living memory*. There was, as I understand it, no memorandum to the effect that our political culture had *been changed* by a process of strategic, top-down redesign. So, much as I might like to, I cannot blame 'a culture change initiative' or, even, Atkinson's 'strategies for success' for the woeful conduct that now shapes public life in Britain. Yet it is clear from the behaviour of our politicians and their advisors that the values which shape conduct in public office have adapted in ways that allow fools and *flâneurs* to hold (elected) office even as they lie, cheat, and bully civil servants.

We could, of course, debate why it is that standards in public life have declined so dramatically – *and I know who I blame* – but the point remains that our experience of Whitehall demonstrates that 'culture' (the everyday interactions which shape *how things get done around here*) is complex, dynamic, negotiable and sometimes just a bit seedy.

And yet . . . the models of culture change which we teach our students remain simplistic, static, top-down in orientation and wilfully blind to the organized profanity that is the workplace. Until now that is . . .

*****

This little book builds upon the critique developed before and upon additional concerns (developed throughout the remainder of this text) to rethink organizational culture. Yet our text is perhaps a little unusual.

At the risk of featuring in *Private Eye's* 'pseuds corner'[3], it may be useful to observe that this little book takes its inspiration from rope-bridge building; principally from the social and technical practices that allow the natives of the Peruvian highlands to construct the crossings that allow movement between the gorges which divide the remote, mountain communities of the Andes. This form of bridge building is, in the highland context of Peru, a communal effort: All those who will benefit from the crossing are, it seems, expected to contribute to the processes that will construct the bridge and are, consequently, obliged to spend many hours collecting long blades of grass which are then twisted and plaited to develop ropes that, when combined, are strong enough to support the passage on foot.

Taking inspiration from this collective endeavour, I will attempt to acknowledge the complexity of the field concerned with culture and its management by developing not a single linear argument but a number of analytical 'threads'. These threads, as we shall see, correspond and will be brought together in our final section. Yet our approach rejects textual linearity in favour of an approach that is, perhaps, more *textile* in nature. As our analysis proceeds, we will combine (and twist) our threads in order to develop an account that, like a good rope, can form a bridge to those concerns that are, too often, beyond the reach of the managerial discourse on culture and change.

To facilitate this (textile) approach, I will:

* Reflect upon the manner in which 'culture' has been framed within the discipline of management.

  In his inaugural professorial lecture, delivered at Leicester University some years ago, my friend and colleague Professor Cliff Oswick observed that the field of management studies is 'in the import business'. In this statement, Professor Oswick reminds us that most of the core ideas which now shape academic discourse in the field of management have been borrowed from other disciplines such as sociology and philosophy.

  In threads two and three, I will consider this cross-border trade as we reflect upon the manner in which 'culture' was constituted by ethnologists and, later, imported into the field of management studies.

* Analyse and account for the entry of 'culture' into the field of management studies.

  It is often suggested that 'organizational culture' a) entered the field of management in the early 1980s and in so doing b) altered our understanding of what it is to be a good manager (Collins, 2021a). This suggestion is not incorrect but it is, as we shall see, far from being the whole truth, because it is clear that the managers and organizational commentators, active in earlier decades, *did* understand that the workplace is shaped *inter alia* by values and by social reciprocities. Acknowledging this, I will develop an account of organizational culture which acknowledges its 'pre-history' (Thompson and McHugh, 1990) *and* its abiding concerns.

* Analyse a small range of those models that have been developed, variously, to explore and to account for the operation of organizational cultures.

  Here, I will focus attention upon the accounts of organizational culture developed by Deal and Kennedy (1982), Schein (1985), Handy ([1978] 2010, 1985), and Hofstede (1980, 1991; Hofstede, Hofstede and Minkov, 2010). I do not suggest that these frameworks offer an exhaustive treatment of culture. I will, however, argue that these models are worthy of analysis, in part, because they are commonly exhibited in texts designed for the education of management students. Yet my analysis is shaped by more than a simple concern with exposition. Having exhibited the models of culture which we routinely teach our students, I will invite a more critical reading. I will argue that the models of culture listed before should be considered to be a) cultural artefacts that some 40 years on from their initial presentation b) might now be re-viewed (Collins and Rainwater, 2005) to offer a fuller reflection

on the nature of organizational culture and its presence within management studies.

• Redeem a cultural appreciation of organizations through an analysis of
those organizational narratives that pursue forms of conduct written out
of the study of organizational culture.

Writing some years ago, the sociologist Wright-Mills (1973)[4] complained that academia had become distanced from its true calling.
Academic sociology, he observed, had developed quantitative survey
techniques and abstract forms of modelling in its attempts to develop a
rigorous appreciation of our organized world. Yet this *rigour*, he suggested, had come at the price of *reality*. Complaining that academic
sociology had made objects of its subjects, Wright-Mills advised
those who would know of the social world and of the affairs of men
and women, more generally, that they should shun textbooks, seek-
ing instead the company of novelists. Taking my cue from Wright-
Mills, I will suggest that stories have the capacity to redeem the study
of organization-as-cultures insofar as they allow us to come to terms
with a range of norms, values and beliefs that, while they plainly shape
conduct, have in effect been excluded from the analytical frame. I will
then conclude with a final thread which in offering a summary of my
core concerns is designed to lash together the threads of argument that
define this little book.

I should warn you, however, that if you are looking for a list; if
you seek an *n*-step guide (Collins, 1998); if you expect this text to
conclude with some glib or programmatic resolution to the problems
that arise when we seek to explore and/or change 'culture', this is not
the book for you. However, if you are frustrated by those accounts of
social organization that claim mastery of the world and yet would deny
your intuitions and experiences of the profane complexity of managerial work, you really should read on.

Notes

1 To conclude a list such as this with the abbreviation 'etc.' is, of course, to assert
   that the situation/problem is so commonly understood that it would be *prolix* to
   offer any more definitive listing of the issues or concerns.
2 This flag becomes 'the Union Jack' only when it is flown by a ship!
3 Pseud's Corner is a regular feature within the fortnightly publication, *Private Eye*.
   This feature lampoons authors for the articulation of prose that is often quite cor-
   rectly taken to be pretentious and/or meaningless.
4 Whyte ([1956] 1961: 95) suggests that Peter Drucker made a similar point in the
   1950s: averring that the most vocational course for a manager would be one in the
   writing of poetry or short stories.

2 Foundations of cultural studies

Introduction

Accounts of organizational culture prepared for students of management typically suggest that managers first, properly, conceived of business organizations as cultures – as social systems with norms, values, beliefs and reciprocal obligations that shape conduct and, consequently, decision-making – in the early 1980s. Indeed, commentators generally acknowledge that the entrance of 'culture' into the discourse of management might be read as a response to the economic crises that shaped the 1970s.

While nodding towards influences that pre-date this decade and while conceding some contest as to the nature of 'culture', it seems to me that textbooks developed for students (see, for example Brown, 1995) and texts prepared for practising managers (see Atkinson, 1997) proceed on the understanding that the *real* business of modern management is to know just enough of 'culture' to be able to engineer a change in its essence and function.

I understand this impetus. Managers are, as Mintzberg (1973) demonstrated so ably, action-oriented people – individuals who are rewarded for initiative – for starting things! Yet in this thread I will argue that, if we are to comprehend the problems that arise when we venture to lead, when we seek to change how people think, feel, speak and act, we will require a historical frame that extends beyond the 1980s. I will pause, therefore, to explore the origins of academic scholarship on 'culture'.

Constituting *Kultur*

Kuper (1996, 1999), a leading social anthropologist who has written extensively on the study of culture(s), notes that the early students of what we now, casually, refer to as 'culture' had first to navigate a path between national traditions and conventions. Indeed, he notes that there were elements within the US academy who were hostile to the term itself, arguing that a concern with *Kultur* indicated support for Germanic scholarly traditions that compared unfavourably to the focus upon 'civilization' that was preferred, for example, by French scholars. Furthermore, Kuper notes that British scholars were wary of both the French and German traditions, in part, because they found it difficult to accept that ranking societies according to their notional development as 'cultures' and/or 'civilizations' was productive.

Kuper observes that it was the sociologist, Talcot Parsons, who pioneered the study of 'culture' in the US academy. Parsons, we should note, was very much influenced by Max Weber, who had suggested that societal beliefs, such as religion, could be used to explain variations in economic development. Building upon Weber's concerns, Parsons developed a cultural reading of economics, framed within an account of 'positivism' (see Burrell and Morgan, 1979). Locating his analytical concerns within positivism, Parsons argued that sociologists should adopt the habits of the natural scientist and in so doing should orient themselves to the acquisition of 'social facts'. To support this agenda, Parsons recruited an inter-disciplinary social science faculty. Ethnologists were recruited to this emerging faculty, Kuper notes, to study 'culture'.

In search of 'culture', the ethnologists recruited by Parsons focused upon symbols and symbolism (e.g. marriage celebrations, funeral *rites*, and culinary and dietary prohibitions). Kuper observes, however, that the ethnologists were very much junior partners in the Parsonian project. Indeed, Kuper tells us that the ethnologists were obliged to accept that they should confine themselves to the study of rites and symbols, ceding the study of social institutions, social structures, and, indeed, social action to their sociological counterparts. Commenting upon the outcome of this division of labour, Kuper (1999) notes that, in the US context, to speak of 'culture' was to suggest an inventory of symbols. These symbols, Kuper acknowledges, clearly described elements of a society but did not really amount to an analytical account of the thoughts, feelings, and values of those under study.

Turning his attention to the British scene, Kuper (1996) observes that the study of 'culture' in the British academy was somewhat less constrained than in America. Nonetheless, he argues that in both Britain and America, the study of thoughts, feelings, and values was shaped by a 'functionalist' approach. This functionalist approach, we should note, tends to assume that the 'culture' under study may be conceived as a unified whole. Proceeding from this position, the functionalist approaches which shape the foundations of British social anthropology have tended to assume that the cultural norms maintained by groupings persist because they perform integrating functions that are, for the collective, socially useful. Later, we will ask: useful for whom? But for the moment, we must continue with our 'origins' story.

Bronsilav Malinowski

Malinowski, a Polish *émigré* working at the London School of Economics, is generally regarded as one of the founding fathers of the British School of social anthropology. Writing in the opening decades of the twentieth century, he observed that, hitherto, knowledge of 'primitive society' had been derived from the experience of missionaries and from those employed within the apparatus of colonial administration. Yet Malinowski complained that the knowledge and understanding developed by these individuals was superficial and unreliable. The testimonials of the missionary and the diaries of the colonial functionary, he warned, encouraged distortion and peddled misinformation because they failed to constitute the world from the native's perspective.

Benedict ([1934] 1989: 48–49) offers a useful summary of the position and the problem facing Malinowski. She warns:

> The classical anthropologists did not write out first-hand knowledge of primitive people. They were armchair students who had at their disposal the anecdotes of travellers and missionaries and the formal and schematic accounts of the early ethnologists. It was possible to trace from these details the distribution of the customs of knocking out teeth, or of divination by entrails, but it was not possible to see how these traits were embedded in different tribes in characteristic configurations that gave form and meaning to the procedures.
>
> (48–49)

To acquire an embedded account and perspective, Malinowski argued that students of social anthropology should a) learn to communicate with 'the native' in the vernacular and should b) choose to live with the tribe under study for an extended period of time so that a deeper and more sensitive appreciation of cultural norms and values might be formed. Yet the fieldwork habits pioneered by Malinowski accepted 'functionalist' ideas as the core organizing principle of his anthropology. Consequently, critics have observed that Malinowski's work finds it difficult to accommodate everyday social dynamics and, hence, struggles to explain and to account for social change. Nonetheless, it is clear that Malinowski's extended fieldwork among, for example, Trobriand Islanders, was able to produce a very human account of his subjects. Indeed, we should note that while his US counterparts were inclined to suggest, for example, that native hostility to economic development signalled 'cultural deficiency', Malinowski insisted that 'native' conduct, while perhaps strange to our eyes, was subject to local concerns and interests which made this both explicable and rational *when taken seriously in its own context.*

Challenging the suggestion that culture, somehow, programmed and *required* particular responses from 'the native', therefore, Malinowski observed that when faced with an obligation, the Trobriand Islander, for example, would behave just as the practising social anthropologist might. In other words, the islander would weigh up the benefits of compliance against the penalties that might be incurred due to a failure to honour the cultural convention in question and would then act in a manner that reflected his/her own concerns and proclivities.

Acknowledging Malinowski's reflexivity, Benedict ([1934] 1989: 56) proposes social anthropology as 'a détour', a visit to those simpler social formations which, because they are unfamiliar and lack the intricacies that define our modern lives, may provide, in any sense, a reflection of the priorities that structure our own interactions. For Benedict, therefore, social anthropology offers a renewed self-knowledge derived from 'the many-sided understanding of a few cultures' (56).

We will return to the issue of self-knowledge as we review the models of organizational culture that students are expected to know and to reproduce. But before we can do this, it will be helpful to consider the manner in which 'culture' entered and altered the field of management. In our next thread, therefore, we will turn our attention to the importation of 'organizational culture' into the field of management studies. As we shall see, the subject of management studies has adopted the language of social anthropology in its discussion of culture but often lacks the reflexivity that Benedict suggests is the gift wrapped within comparative study.

3   The pre-history of organizational culture

Introduction

Writing a preface for the 1959 edition of Benedict's ([1934] 1989: xi) *Patterns of Culture*, Margaret Mead pays compliment to her colleague:

> When Ruth Benedict began her work in anthropology in 1921, the term 'culture' as we use it today for the systematic body of learned behaviour which is transmitted from parents to children, was part of the vocabulary of a small and technical group of professional anthropologists. That today the modern world is on such easy terms with the concept of culture, that the words 'in our culture' slip from the lips of educated men and women as effortlessly as do the phrases that refer to period and place is in very great part due to this book.

Benedict's work is a classic text on culture. Indeed, her work rewards, especially, those who choose to re-read her reflections on – not cultural types – but patterns of culture. Yet Benedict's text is, I fear, now largely ignored by those who are concerned to channel and to change organizational or corporate cultures. Instead, those with an interest in organizational culture – and to be clear, for most the interest in 'organizational culture' generally resolves to a position which articulates a desire to change norms and values in the name of customer needs and competitive imperatives – generally proceed from a reading of the works of Deal and Kennedy (1982, 1999). This choice of reading materials is readily understandable. The works of Deal and Kennedy have become an 'obligatory passage point' (see Latour, 1987) for students, a piece of knowledge that all are expected, at least, to nod towards as they develop their preferred accounts of 'culture' and 'change'. Yet it is worth observing that while the text prepared by Deal and Kennedy has become (if only through repetition) foundational to the discussion of 'organizational culture', others *had* previously recognized that the workplace might usefully be configured in cultural terms. In the 1970s Harrison (1972) and later Handy ([1978] 2010), for example both developed typologies of organizational culture. Yet other contributions pre-date even these texts. Indeed, it is clear that F. W. Taylor's (1911) 'scientific management' was, at root, an exercise in what we would now term as 'culture change'.

Taylorism

F. W. Taylor's (1911) approach to industrial engineering is centrally concerned with efficiency and with the development of an approach to management, which is designed to remove unnecessary movement and duplication of effort. Indeed, Taylorism is often referred to as one of a group of approaches focused upon the study of 'time and motion'.

Taylor argued that the observation of motion and the measurement of time would allow managers to ascertain the single best way to do just about any job. Yet, he warned that the pursuit of scientific management would require broader organizational changes, designed to sweep away outmoded working practices. Explaining the need for this fundamental change, Taylor argued that, left to their own devices, employees tended to arrange their working practices to reflect the customs and traditions that had been passed down through previous generations. He complained, however, that these traditional practices were alarmingly inefficient and ill-suited to modern factory systems of working. To secure greater efficiencies in the management of work, therefore, Taylor argued that the control over the design and management of work would have to be wrested from employees. Taylorist systems of working, therefore, increased specialization in two senses. First, there would be a change in the responsibilities of management and workers. Managers would specialize in work design, taking responsibility for planning tasks and for designing systems of work, while workers would be expected to carry out their duties according to managerial instruction. The second specialization required by Taylorism relates to the actual tasks that the workers would be instructed to perform.

Under traditional craft systems of working, employees often enjoy considerable discretion in the performance of their work. Skilled or 'craft workers', for example, tend to experience variety in the work that they perform, often undertaking all of the operations necessary for the completion of any particular product. Taylor, however, regarded this approach to working as wasteful and inefficient. Within Taylorized systems of working, therefore, the many tasks previously performed by a single worker were sub-divided and reallocated among groups of semi-skilled workers.

Crainer (1997: 50–51) offers a useful illustration of the specialized working processes (and technologies) that now deliver our manufactured goods. Discussing Henry Ford's system of car production, which made extensive use of 'time and motion' while adding an additional innovation, namely the moving production line, Crainer invites us to consider the organizational transformation associated with labour specialization. Henry Ford, as Crainer tells us, 'calculated that the production of his Model T car required 7882 different operations. Of these 949 required "strong, able-bodied and practically physically perfect men" and 3338 required "ordinary physical strength." The remainder, said Ford, could be undertaken by "women or older children" and "we found that 670 could be filled by legless men, 2637 by one-legged men, two by armless men, 715 by one-armed men and 10 by blind men"'.

Taylor is, of course, associated with an approach to management that is 'hard', cold, and rational in its approach. Yet, contemporary accounts of the development and implementation of Taylorism demonstrate that scientific management was (of course) developed within a social–cultural context that carried ramifications for its application and implementation. Indeed, commentators remind us that workers often combined to oppose Taylorism and (incidentally) to keep their workmates in line. Braverman (1974), for example, notes that, as collectives, coal-miners often simply refused to assist 'time and motion' study operatives in their endeavours, choosing to sit on their shovels whenever they were subjected to the scrutiny of work study engineers.

Highlighting the social organization necessary to maintain opposition to developments such as Taylorism, Buchanan and Huczynski (1997) reflect upon the manner in which groups within the workplace would label (and punish) those inclined to collaborate with the advocates of 'scientific management'. Thus, Buchanan and Huczynski note that those who allowed time and motion specialists to review and to time their work were labelled as 'chisellers', whereas those who broke group norms by working at a pace that would attract the attention of the time and motion engineers were labelled as 'rate-busters'. Both chisellers and rate-busters, we should note, were often subjected to group sanctions and punishments.

This inner, social world of Taylorism demonstrates that, despite what you may have been told about Taylor's cold-hearted rationalism, the implementation of his 'time and motion' approach was inherently 'social' inasmuch as it was built upon an attempt to convince employees that mutual prosperity could be assured *if only* workers would entrust management with the tasks associated with job design. In other words cold, hard scientific management was, at root, a culture change programme . . . albeit one that was, paradoxically, designed to break down the social solidarities that employees had formed in the workplace.

Some decades on from the publication of Taylor's (1911) book on the principles of scientific management, those leading the Hawthorne Studies on the links between productivity, environmental conditions, and fatigue demonstrated a similar awareness of the manner in which social understandings and obligations shape conduct at work. Indeed, it is worth noting that the researchers operating within the Hawthorne factory had actually recruited a social anthropologist from Britain as they attempted to come to terms with what would, in time, become framed as the social system of the workplace. Unlike Taylor, however, the Hawthorne researchers took a more positive view of workplace cultures. Where Taylorism sought to break down collectives, the Hawthorne researchers chose to highlight, explicitly, the extent to which 'social factors' might intervene positively within the workplace, allowing groups to overcome fatigue and/or poor working conditions.

Yet, the Hawthorne researchers struggled to understand the workplace from 'the native's perspective' and tended to invoke something akin to the 'cultural deficiency' argument invoked by US ethnologists as they attempted to explain key aspects of worker conduct. Confronted, for example, by the knowledge that factory workers who were employed on 'piece rate' chose to hide the work that they had completed, the researchers decided that the employees simply lacked a basic grasp of economics. This observation would be laughable, I suggest were it not insulting! Indeed, a more sensitive reading of the conduct observed demonstrates that, not only is this worker conduct based upon an understanding of economics, it is, in fact, founded upon a long-term understanding of the mechanisms shaping the labour market. Thus, we should note that the employees paid on a 'piece work' were routinely 'laid off' or, perhaps less euphemistically, were sent home with no pay, or minimal pay, when the organization experienced a periodic dip in demand. When the market recovered, these employees would be recalled to work and might, then, be asked to work at an especially high pace, for example, to accommodate an urgent order. This brief period of working would, of course, pay well. But it would hardly compensate for historical and subsequent periods of inactivity consequent upon an approach to labour management based around periodic lay-offs. Over time, therefore, the employees observed within the Hawthorne studies had simply learned that working at the pace demanded by their employer was economically irrational. Reflecting upon this activity from 'the native perspective', Wright (1994) argues that those employees who had been observed to hide their production were acting rationally; they were, in effect, smoothing output in an attempt to maximize their incomes in the long term. In short, Wright suggests that, it was the academics who were culturally deficient. It was, she argues, the ever-so-clever researchers, who had failed to grasp the brutal economics of the workplace and the rational choice-making of their subjects!

It is of course important that we understand that those whom we tend to regard as the founding fathers of modern management had, however grudgingly, recognized that the workplace is, in some sense, a culture – social system regulated by shared concerns, common orientations, and tacit understandings. Yet we must also acknowledge the work of those who did *clearly and explicitly* seek to navigate work organizations in cultural terms.

The changing culture of the factory

Eliot Jaques (1951) was, perhaps, the first commentator to speak of 'culture' in the context of work organizations. Offering a case study of the Glacier Metal Company – famous both for the manufacture of ball bearings and for its willingness to collaborate with academics – Jaques identifies tensions within the ranks of management, which mock Atkinson's simple devotion to idea that organizational goals are, somehow, singular and all-encompassing. Indeed, Jaques notes that disharmony between managers related, in part, to tensions arising around overlapping systems of 'executive' and 'consultative' systems of management. In addition, Jaques highlights confusion as to the role of the local Managing Director who was, at that time, also General Manager of the company's London factory and Chairman of the Board of Directors. Furthermore, he highlights tensions between 'line managers' and a new cadre of 'executive managers' who had been installed within the company.

Defining his engagement with the social system of the factory, Jaques (1951: 251) offers an account of culture that would have been (painfully) familiar to Taylor's 'time and motion' specialists. Thus, he observes that

> the culture of the factory is its customary and traditional way of thinking and doing of things, which is shaped to a greater or lesser degree by all its members, and which new members must learn and at least partially accept, in order to be accepted into service in the firm.

This definition is significant for it makes it clear that, far from being a dead weight or a crushing and unavoidable template for thought and action, 'the culture of the factory' is something that we can accept partially and conditionally. Returning to our earlier discussion of Taylorism, therefore, it is now worth pointing out that while opposition to scientific management was based, often, upon the punishment of those who engaged in chiselling and rate-busting, at least some of those present within the workplace clearly felt able to go their own way, culturally, and in so doing did choose, either, to collaborate with the time and motion specialists or to work at a pace that would invite re-timing and, inevitably, a reduction in the piece rate. Furthermore, the account of culture preferred by Jaques reminds us that while the social structure of the workplace is, so often, a target for change, it is also a source of collective power. Thus, it is clear that in their opposition to the individualized approach to management pursued in the name of Taylorism, the coal miners, for example, invoked social solidarities, crystallized around customary patterns of thought and action, in order to defend their occupational culture against the incursions of management.

Yet, while it would be accurate to suggest that the recognition of the managerial significance of 'organizational culture' can a) be traced back to the early years of the twentieth century and did b) continue into the 1950s it is, nonetheless, true that managerial interest in all things cultural c) accelerated in the early 1980s and d) has its roots in the socio-economic crisis that rocked the US economy during the 1970s.

In our next thread, we will address this concern as we consider what is often termed the cultural turn in management.

4 Models of organizational culture

Introduction

In this thread, we will offer reflections on the manner in which notions of 'culture' and 'cultural change' entered and altered the field of management studies in the 1980s. We will suggest that while commentators had previously discussed business organizations in cultural terms, it was not until the 1980s that this mode of expression truly became common currency in business school lecture theatres and company boardrooms. But to explain this shift, we must pause to consider the crisis that gripped the United States in the 1970s and the reaction to this.

The crisis of the 1970s

During the late 1970s and early 1980s, the US economy faced what economists have dubbed 'stagflation' – a surprising (and alarming) combination of price inflation and economic stagnation which led to double digit rates of inflation, unemployment, and bank interest. These conditions – the worst endured in a generation – were especially problematic for American commentators, however, because they contrasted so starkly with the experience of the Japanese economy which had continued to prosper throughout this period.

Documenting the continuing rise of the Japanese economy, Pascale and Athos ([1981] 1986: 20) offer a very useful indication of the threat perceived:

> In 1980 Japan's GNP was third highest in the world and if we extrapolate current trends it would be number one by the year 2000. A country the size of Montana, Japan has virtually no physical resources, yet it supports over 115 million people (half the population of the United States), exports $75 billion worth more goods than it imports and has

an investment rate as well as a GNP growth rate which is twice that of the United States. Japan has come to dominate in one selected industry after another – eclipsing the British in motorcycles, surpassing the Germans and the Americans in automobile production, wrestling leadership from the Germans and the Swiss in watches, cameras and optical instruments and overcoming the United States' historical dominance in businesses as diverse as steel, shipbuilding, pianos, zippers and consumer electronics.

Accounting for this success, Pascale and Athos argued that the root cause of Japan's growing economic dominance was, primarily, managerial. The Japanese, the authors argued, had secured a level of cultural control unimagined in America. This cultural proficiency, Pascale and Athos reasoned, had allowed Japanese organizations to reduce the direct control mechanisms favoured by Taylorist systems of working in favour of an approach that sought and secured employee commitment to customers, innovation, and change.

Pursuing this distinctive managerial capability, Pascale and Athos and Peters and Waterman (1982) worked together to develop what has come to be known as the McKinsey 7-S framework (see Figure 4.1). This, now very familiar model suggests that the work of management involves the combination of 'hard', technical functions and 'soft' or people-oriented processes. Drawing upon this *heuristic,* Peters and Waterman argued that American managers had downplayed the importance of human factors at work and, consequently, needed to re-balance the hard-S factors and the soft-S factors of business in order to ensure that US corporations would have cultures appropriate to the business needs of the 1980s and beyond.

While organizational culture clearly formed a core component of the analyses developed by Pascale and Athos ([1981] 1986) and Peters and Waterman (1982), the work of Deal and Kennedy (1982) is notable insofar as it a) offered a lengthy description of artefacts, rituals, and cultural symbols while offering b) perhaps, the most concise 'definition' of organizational culture. Thus, Deal and Kennedy suggest that culture may be condensed to a simple statement of fact. Culture is, they assert, simply 'how we do things around here' (4).

This is, of course, rather a long way from a full definition of culture, but this statement does at least demonstrate a useful intuition about *what* people do at work and *why*. Thus, the shorthand of Deal and Kennedy suggests that culture *is a pattern of action*, which is to say that we can come to know of cultural norms and organizational values through sustained reflection on what people say and do.

The analysis developed by Deal and Kennedy also makes it clear, however, that 'culture' is also to be regarded as *a pattern for action* insofar as

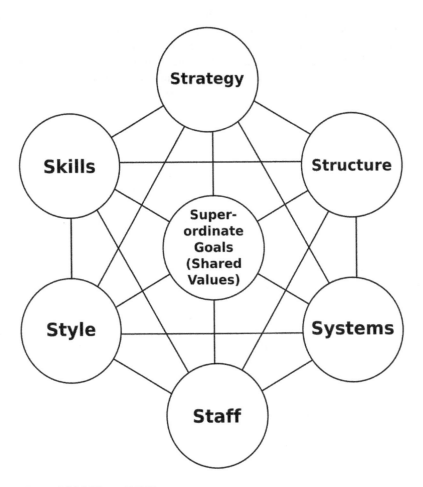

Figure 4.1 McKinsey 7-S Diagram

behaviours and policies express interests, priorities, and matters of concern that shape our conduct, whether or not we choose to acknowledge this fact. Thus, the cultural *norms* visible, for example, in the manner in which people dress and in the terms they use when they address one another offer some indication of what people regard as useful and proper within this context – in short their *values*.

Parker (1993: 4–5) allows us to see both faces of culture rather well in his account of the speech patterns that shape conduct and interactions in the city of Belfast. Noting the religious and political divisions more or less opaque to outsiders, which shape daily life in Belfast, Parker reminds us that the *patterns of action* he observed on 'first contact' are underpinned by *patterns for action* that shape how the people of this city think, feel, act, and indeed interact with one another. As we shall see, Parker also reminds us that in some settings, social interactions may be inherently risky with, for example, small changes in word-choice or inflexion marking you as an outsider or, worse, 'other':

> If you are Protestant and 'British', you'll always call the second biggest city in Northern Ireland 'Londonderry': if you're catholic and/ or Nationalist, you'll only refer to it as 'Derry'. Nationalists and Catholics speak of 'the North', Ireland or, intentionally aggressive, 'the Six Counties'. 'Northern Ireland' and 'Ulster' are Protestant terminology: and to speak of 'the Province' in front of a Nationalist is provocative, even if it wasn't intended. . . . Catholics and particularly Republicans never talk about 'the Troubles' – they use the blunter 'the war' or 'the struggles'. Even in the *minutiae* of pronunciation there are giveaways: the Department of Health and Social Security's initials are pronounced DHSS by Protestants, but by Catholics 'D Haitch SS'. So too with the IRA: more correctly 'The Provisional IRA', its members are only called the 'Provos' by Protestants: to Republicans, Nationalists and Catholics they're 'the Provies'; the slightly changed sound with its more moderating softness perhaps revealing something else as well. These are only some of the more obvious pointers. But in every conversation there'll come the faintest of suppressed grimaces, or the slightest flicker in the eye as a 'wrong' word is used revealing you to be one of the 'others'.

Deal and Kennedy are rather pre-occupied by the symbols and artefacts that shape our organizational lives. Such symbols, rituals, totems, and artefacts they suggest may be combined in so many different ways that each organizational culture may be considered to be unique. Accounting for these differences, they suggest that organizational cultures have developed and have adapted, primarily, to address product and market characteristics. In the light of these contingencies, the authors suggest that four ideal types of culture may be found.

To suggest that these types are 'ideal' is not to suggest, of course, that they are in any sense perfect or even good. Some cultural variants discussed by the authors, as we shall see, in a later thread seem pretty toxic! Instead, the observation of an 'ideal type' is an attempt to suggest that, in this case, the culture under study represents a useful adaptation – a good fit for the contingency that defines its shape and function.

The four culture types described by Deal and Kennedy are to be read therefore as responses:

1) To the degree of risk associated with the organization's activities
2) To the speed with which the organization receives feedback from the marketplace

The tough guy, macho culture

The first of the four ideal types identified by Deal and Kennedy is, they tell us, associated with organizations engaged, for example, in investment banking and advertising (see Figure 4.2). These production contexts, the authors tell us, are inherently risky. Furthermore, the feedback on decision-making

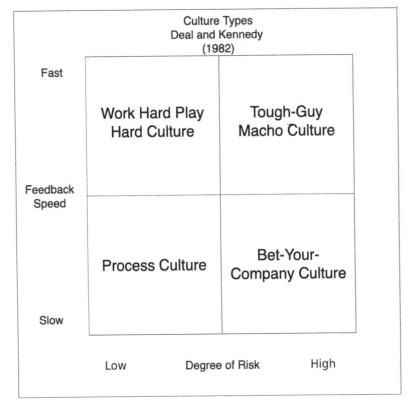

Figure 4.2 Deal and Kennedy Model of Culture

available to organizational members within such contexts is rapid and, where negative, highly damaging to the organization as a whole. Noting that these cultures value risk-taking and are highly individualist, Deal and Kennedy dub the first of their ideal types the 'tough guy, macho culture'.

The work hard/play hard culture

The second of the ideal types identified by Deal and Kennedy is labelled the 'work hard/ play hard' culture. Organizations working within this context, we are told, experience rapid feedback on their decision-making but, unlike the 'tough guy, macho culture', do not experience such a high degree of risk. The 'work hard/play hard' culture therefore might be thought as typical of those organizations involved in, for example, car sales. Deal and Kennedy suggest that key characteristics of this culture include 'presenteeism' and the obligation to socialize with colleagues during personal leisure time.

The bet-your-company culture

The third ideal type suggested by Deal and Kennedy is labelled the 'bet-your-company culture'. Individuals within this production context are, like those involved in investment banking, for example, engaged in high-risk endeavours. Yet, unlike the case of investment banking, the feedback on decision-making in this context is slow, and the pay-off on the bets made is realized only in the long term. Deal and Kennedy argue that organizations involved in these endeavours – and contemporary examples might include the production of commercial aircraft, drug development, and, perhaps, private space exploration programmes such as SpaceX – tend to develop cultures which embrace a long-term time frame and in so doing encourage employees to commit to a stable and enduring guiding philosophy or ethos.

Process cultures

The fourth ideal type identified by Deal and Kennedy is labelled a 'process culture'. The organizations within this category, which are, we are told, often involved in the retail sector or in the insurance business, are said to face low levels of risk associated with any individual decision. Furthermore, they are said to receive feedback on their actions over a very long time frame. Indeed, Deal and Kennedy suggest that more junior employees in this context often receive no feedback on their endeavours and as a consequence may suffer neurotic disorders.

Deal and Kennedy, we should note, do tend to discuss 'organizational cultures' from the top-down and in so doing suggest that cultures have a unifying capability. Yet they do concede that that in certain circumstances, some of their ideal types may be found side-by-side within certain organizations. For example it is perfectly possible to imagine the 'bet-your-company culture' existing side-by-side with the 'work hard/play hard' culture. In the automobile business, for example, those who lead production and design decisions might be said to live within a 'bet-your-company' context since they are obliged to make billion dollar choices that will take some years to pay-off, whereas the sales personnel employed within the dealer network might be said to work within a 'work hard/play hard' culture.

Others who have acknowledged the presence of different cultural 'types' within a single organization are, however, less persuaded by the suggestion that organizational culture is, in fact, a source of common purpose and unification. Bob Lutz (2011), former Vice-Chairman of *General Motors,* offers a cultural account of this car company which, like that of Jaques, highlights tensions between managerial specialists.

Car guys and bean counters

Bob Lutz offers a pretty colourful appreciation of the car manufacturing business. Indeed, he is quite unable to disguise his dislike of accountants and MBA generalists and so offers us instruction in the everyday prejudices that so often define our workplace cultures.

Lutz insists that *General Motors* prospered when it a) placed engineers and proper 'car guys' (*whatever these may be*) at the strategic apex of the organization and when it b) allowed design matters and aesthetic concerns to take priority. Indeed, he suggests that the physical separation of organizational departments (with 'design' being located in Detroit and the 'accountants' housed in New York) had for a time worked to insulate the true 'car guys' within *General Motors* from the MBA-trained generalists who, he protests, made cost-cutting their one priority. Lutz does concede, of course, that the designers had been arrogant and were often hubristic as regards emerging competitors such as Japan; nonetheless, he protests that, when protected from the emergent 'generalist' managers and 'bean counters', the 'proper' 'car guys' had been allowed to build vehicles with character – cars that the customer actually wanted to buy.

Of course, we might venture that Lutz's headline attack on the 'bean counters' is unfair and simplifies the complex geo-politics of the global car business.[1] And these complaints are undoubtedly truthful. Yet the core point remains. Despite the suggestion that 'culture' is a unifying force, the work of Lutz (2011) shows, in relief, the cultural prejudices, tensions, and turf wars that persist among even the most senior managers.

This is a point we will return to; for the moment, however, we must conclude our reflections on the work of Deal and Kennedy for as we shall see these authors *are* inclined to view culture from the top-down and in so doing tend to be dismissive of those who would give voice to plurality.

Strong and weak cultures

While suggesting the presence of four ideal cultural types, Deal and Kennedy (in common with Atkinson (1997)) suggest that some of these cultures may perform in a sub-optimal fashion. Thus, the authors highlight the presence of 'strong' and 'weak' variations of their ideal types'. Strong cultures, it seems, are those that are controlled from the top and aligned with the interests of the business. Those cultures that are, somehow, less enthralled by managerial projections of 'organizational needs' and which are, consequently, more difficult to control and channel are, we are told, 'weak'.

This terminology, of course, adds little in the way of analytical clarity or sophistication, but it is nonetheless powerful in political terms. Thus the perceived duality between strong and weak, vibrant and moribund, and good and bad cultures offers the whip hand to those actors – whether they be 'car guys', 'bean counters', or, worst of all it seems, 'MBA-trained generalists' – who would project their own interests as being representative of the common good.

Handy's cultural types

Handy's ([1978] 2010, 1985) re-working of Harrison's reflections on culture also produces four 'types'. Handy's cultural types however are less driven by environmental factors. Indeed, they may be said to be, at one level, embodiments of their founders' personalities. The four types highlighted by Handy are depicted as follows:

* The power culture

   Handy depicts the power culture as a web with of course a central point from which all power to make decisions within 'the organization' is derived (see Figure 4.3). The lines emanating from this central point represent the specialist and/or functional components (such as HR, manufacturing etc.) upon which the organization depends. This cultural formation, we should note, is not unlike the macho culture described by Deal and Kennedy insofar as relations between individuals may be

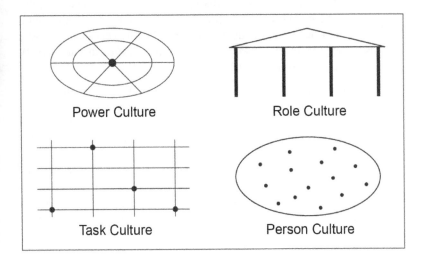

Figure 4.3 Handy's Models of Culture

abrasive and are defined, Handy warns us by a focus upon ends *even* if the means may be questionable.

Handy suggests that the power culture allows for a rapid response to problems and opportunities. Yet, he warns that these cultural forms may prove less productive in the long term. Thus, he suggests that power cultures may find it difficult to maintain the services of their middle-ranking employees. These individuals, he suggests, soon tire of the poor conduct exhibited by their superiors and seek employment elsewhere. Recognizing this, Handy suggests that power cultures may find it difficult to secure their own social reproduction.

The film *The Devil Wears Prada,* which was released in 2006 and is adapted from the book of the same name (Weisberger, 2003) offers, I believe, a good example of the manner in which so-called power cultures act to control and (often) to demotivate subordinates. Indeed, in the extract given later, it soon becomes clear that the influence of Miranda Priestly (played by Meryl Streep) extends far beyond the fashion magazine that she so plainly dominates. In one notable exchange between Priestly and her assistant, Andrea Sachs (played by Anne Hathaway), the junior partner is publicly rebuked. This exchange, a key feature of the film that was not, in fact, a component of the original novel, is precipitated because Sachs finds the manner in which Priestly and other employees of the magazine fuss over 'a pile of stuff' and the minor details of fashion, literally, laughable. Stung by this small but public indiscretion, Priestly turns upon Sachs – her choice of clothing and indeed her sense of self. While continuing to select clothing and accessories for a scheduled feature and while continuing to issue instructions to others (acknowledged by the *ellipses* in our extract), Priestly challenges her junior:

> You go to your closet and you select, I don't know, that lumpy blue sweater because you are trying to tell the world that you take yourself too seriously to care about what you put on your back . . . what you don't know is that sweater is not just blue; it's not turquoise or lapis, it's actually cerulean. And you're also blithely unaware of the fact that in 2002 Oscar de La Renta did a collection of cerulean gowns and then I think it was Yves Saint Laurent, wasn't it, who showed cerulean military jackets . . . and then cerulean quickly showed up in the collections of eight different designers and then it filtered down through the department stores and then trickled on down into some tragic, casual corner where you, no doubt, fished it out of some clearance bin. However that blue represents some millions of dollars and countless jobs and it's sort of comical how you think you've made some sort of choice that exempts you from the fashion industry when, in fact, you're wearing a sweater that was selected for you by the people in this room – from a pile of stuff

- The role culture

The role culture may be said to be a classic bureaucracy such as that identified by Weber. In the role culture, individuals are recruited bureaucratically. In other words, employees are selected according to the knowledge, skills, and qualifications they possess. Where individuals within a power culture operate 'charismatically', the actors within the role culture are recruited to fulfil technical and functional roles on the basis of their acquired qualifications. Communication within role cultures is, primarily, vertical (until at least the strategic apex where information may flow horizontally) with individuals and teams operating, largely, as separate silos.

Role cultures are driven by rules and procedures. This, we should note, provides a stable and reliable operating regime. These cultures, it is suggested, however, do tend to respond slowly to problems and challenges and as a consequence may miss out on opportunities seized by the charismatics operating within, for example, power cultures.

- The task culture

Handy represents the task culture as a lattice. Here, individuals derive their authority from expertise much as they do, for example, within role cultures. Yet, unlike the case of the role culture, the voice and

discretion enjoyed by individuals within this formation is not depen-
dent upon their position within a bureaucratic hierarchy. Indeed, task
cultures are said to be characterized by high levels of functional col-
laboration throughout the organization. Here 'the task', rather than 'the
process', is key. Task cultures, therefore, tend to short-circuit the procedures and reporting relationships developed within role cultures and
in so doing often produce speedy organizational responses to problems
and rapid, product prototypes. That said, those task cultures that are
actively hostile to procedures may find it difficult to transfer learning
from one project to another and may find it difficult to codify those
processes that serve them well. Task cultures, therefore, may become
over-reliant on a small core of individuals who, in effect, constitute the
organization's memory and core competence.

- The person culture

  Handy represents the person culture as a cloud or as a loose cluster of
  individuals. An example of a person culture would be, Handy suggests,
  the 'legal chambers' upon which much of the British legal system
  depends. Traditional 'legal chambers' are, in effect, loose coalitions
  of highly trained individuals – barristers who have come together so
  that they might share office and administrative costs. In this setting, the
  'chambers' may be an organization in name only because the barristers
  (in our example) continue to act throughout as independent practitioners. Viewed from the perspective of the barrister, therefore, the culture
  of 'chambers' may appear to be highly fluid and pretty disorganized.
  However, it is also worth noting that, when viewed from the perspective of the pupil (legal trainee) or clerk, the legal chambers may have
  the character of a role culture!

  Handy suggests that each of these types of culture might be associated with a Greek god:

  - The power or club culture Handy associates with the king of the
    gods Zeus.
  - The role culture, Handy tells us, is associated with Apollo, who is
    of course the god of order and rules.
  - The task culture is, in contrast, associated with Athena, the energetic
    warrior goddess who seeks, always, opportunity and advantage.
  - The person or cluster culture is, Handy tells us, associated with
    Dionysus, the garrulous god of wine and song.

Patterns of culture

Benedict ([1934] 1989: 228) has also built an analysis of culture around
an account of the Greek gods. Yet, she is sceptical of the suggestion that

culture may, usefully, be rendered into a number of archetypes. Indeed, she warns that '[i]t would be absurd to cut every culture down to the Procrustean bed of some catchword or categorization'.

Benedict suggests, instead, that we should look for and should focus upon patterns of culture. These are, she warns us, not 'a fixed constellation of traits' (238).

Highlighting three patterns of culture associated, respectively, with Apollonian, Dionysian, and with 'paranoid' beliefs and interactions, Benedict ([1934] 1989: 238) warns us that '[e]ach one is an empirical characterization, and probably is not duplicated in its entirety anywhere else in the world'.

Elaborating on each of these patterns of culture, Benedict reminds us that the cultures of the Americas that she would use to improve our own self-knowledge are inherently dynamic. For example she documents the development of the Ghost Dance among the tribes of the US plains during the 1870s. Benedict situates the development of this new dance and its associated clothing and rituals as a spontaneous response to threat and crisis. Yet, Benedict is also keen to point out that cultural changes such as the Ghost Dance are themselves culturally located and are enacted differently according to cultural obligations. Indeed, she observes that compared to the natives of the plains, spontaneous cultural change among the *Pueblos* tended to be smaller and more marginal, in part, because tribal elders had to be consulted, for example, on mooted changes to dances, on the meaning of 'visions', and on the role and function of shared rituals.

Benedict suggests that the patterns of culture, which she labels Apollonian, are notable for their moderation, sobriety, and self-abasement. Dionysian cultural patterns are, in contrast, remarkable for the exuberant manner in which they express their joy. Where Apollonian patterns of culture are suspicious of those who voice leaderly ambitions, the Dionysian pattern is uninhibited, boastful, and inclined to the consumption of intoxicants.

In war, those from an Apollonian culture will, of course, engage in combat and will kill their enemies as a duty. Those from a Dionysian cultural pattern, however, are observed to kill joyously. Here, triumphs are celebrated exuberantly, and captives are tortured horribly. This joyous killing and torture, however, exacts a cultural price, for those of a Dionysian cultural pattern tend to live in worlds marked by contamination and supernatural fear. In Dionysian cultural patterns therefore, funeral rites are rituals designed to placate the spirits, atone for excess, and purify earthly concerns, whereas in Apollonian patterns, funeral rites are more straightforwardly designed to allow expressions of loss and grief.

Benedict focuses attention on the Dobuans for her case study of the paranoid cultural pattern. About the Dobuans who live on an island located in Papua New Guinea, Benedict ([1934] 1989: 131) tells us that they

amply deserve the character they are given by neighbours. They are lawless
and treacherous. Every man's hand is against every other man. . . . Dobu
has no chiefs. It certainly has no political organization. In a strict sense it
has no legality. And this is not because the Dobuan lives in a state of anar-
chy, Rousseau's 'natural man' as yet unhampered by the social contract,
but because the social forces which obtain in Dobu put a premium upon
ill-will and treachery and make them the recognized virtues of society

Benedict (1989: 131) points out, however, that there are cultural limitations to the expression of ill-will and treachery even within this society. She
tells us that Dobu society is 'arranged in concentric circles within each of
which traditional forms of hostility are allowed'.

Contrasting the Dobuans with those tribes associated with Apollonian
and Dionysian patterns, Benedict tells us that these south-sea islanders
inhabit a magical world but not a religious one. There are, therefore, no
evil spirits to placate as in the Dionysian pattern. And there are, she notes,
no ancestors who must be pleased to bring forth rain or healthy off-spring
as in the Apollonian frame. When sailing in calmed waters, for example,
the Dobuans 'believe about wind, as they believe about all other events of
existence, that it arises from no other source than magic' (Benedict, [1934]
1989: 157) and is a product of some rival's ill-will or treachery.

Kuehling (2005) protests, however, that Benedict overemphasizes the
aggression of the Dobuans. She highlights, instead, the poverty, the margin-
alization, and the earlier status as indentured labourers, which the Dobuans
endured as factors which explain their cosmology. Nevertheless, Benedict's
comparison of cultural patterns remains illuminating. It continues to invite
self-reflection and, crucially, reminds us of the presence of cultural change
and cultural negotiation even in those societies hitherto taken to be 'primitive' and unchanged throughout human history.

Schein's cultural layers

Schein's (1985) account of culture is, perhaps, more elaborate than that
detailed by Deal and Kennedy (1982) and Handy ([1978] 2010, 1985).
Indeed, where Deal and Kennedy seem content to develop an inventory of
symbols and a plausible (if speculative) cultural typology, Schein is keener
to explore the social-psychology of culture.

Schein's analysis is similar to that of Hall (1976) insofar as both insist
that true cultural awareness develops from a consideration of that which
often cannot be observed directly. In an attempt to convey this understanding, Hall encourages us to think of culture as being like an iceberg insofar
as most of it is obscured from view. Echoing Hall's (1976) analysis, Schein
argues that 'culture' has three levels. The top level of culture, he suggests,

includes all of those things inventoried by Deal and Kennedy (1982). Thus, Schein tells us that organizations, in effect, display cultural artefacts such as stories, myths, jokes, metaphors, rites, rituals, ceremonies, heroes, and symbolic elements which may observed directly (see Figure 4.4). These components, while generally interesting and often intriguing remain, Schein tells us, superficial manifestations of culture that are underpinned by a second deeper level, composed of beliefs, values, and attitudes. These second-level cultural aspects cannot be observed directly although they

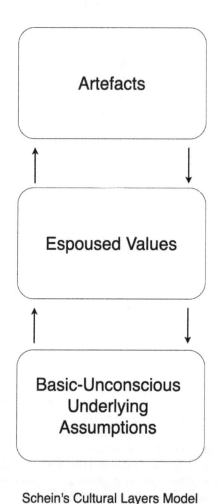

Schein's Cultural Layers Model

Figure 4.4 Schein's Layers Diagram

may be inferred from the behaviours observed in the first level. For example the cultural *norms* manifest in the manner in which people dress and in the terms they use when they address one another may be constituted as evidence of deeper *values* as to what is right and proper. In turn, these *values* may be said to reflect a core set of *beliefs*. I will use a religious example in an attempt to pull these elements together. Since I was raised as a Catholic in Scotland, I will call upon my own biographical knowledge to offer a general illustration of the relationship between norms, values, and beliefs. You may attempt to do likewise from the perspective of your own religious teaching or indeed from a more secular or 'humanist' perspective.

Piecing together my long since abandoned religious education, therefore, it seems to me that belief in the God of the *New Testament* should lead you to hold values associated with neighbourliness and reciprocity such that your conduct will demonstrate that you meet friends and strangers on the same terms, offering to all others the courtesy you would, yourself, hope to receive.

Schein argues that the third and deepest level of culture is concerned with the basic or foundational assumptions which explain and account for human nature and human activity within its environment. Elaborating upon the implications of his modelling, Schein (1985: 6) argues that the term culture 'should be reserved for the deeper level of *basic assumptions* and *beliefs* that are shared by members of an organization, that operate unconsciously, and that define in a basic "taken-for-granted" fashion an organization's view of itself and its environment' (original emphasis).

This assertion is, of course, useful at one level. It is, for example, clear that we do not generally spend much time thinking about the orientations that shape our day-to-day interactions. As Burrell (1997) observes, we tend to think *with* rather than *about* our beliefs! Equally, Schein's account of culture reminds us that the *patterns of action*, which we are able to observe within the workplace (for example), do tend to be rooted in fairly deep-seated *patterns for action* which, in embodying beliefs and values, act to set priorities and so define what is 'good', what is 'bad', who is on 'the inside', and who is on the 'outside'.

We will offer a more critical reading of Schein's (1985) analysis in our fifth thread. For the moment, however, we will conclude this segment of our track with reflections on the work of Hofstede (1980, 1991; Hofstede, Hofstede and Minkov, 2010).

Hofstede and national cultures

Hofstede concedes that nations and national boundaries are often arbitrary divisions – lines drawn on maps by colonial empires, imperial powers, and/

or the victors of some local war. And in this Hofstede is correct. The map of Africa, for example, is covered in straight lines which seem to show little respect for topographical contours. Furthermore, it is striking that following the dissolution of Yugoslavia and the break-up of the Soviet Union in the early 1990s, maps drawn in 1919 were suddenly more accurate than those composed in the 1980s. Nonetheless, Hofstede insists that there exist enduring national characteristics (loosely reflective of the lines on a map) which shape business cultures such that the prevailing norms and values at work in, say Germany, are typically rather different to those that prevail in, say the United States.

Hofstede based his initial research upon questionnaires distributed in 1967 and in 1973 to employees working within IBM subsidiaries across 66 countries. In retrospect, we are told, Hofstede came to realize that these surveys offered data that might be pertinent in understanding the 'values', which he suggests underpins culturally appropriate conduct.

Hofstede reasoned that the values of IBM's employees were shaped *organizationally, occupationally*, and *nationally*. He argued that the culture of IBM was common across all 66 subsidiaries and so could not be considered to be a source of variance. Furthermore, he tells us that he took steps to match responses to his survey by 'occupation' so that this too might be excluded as a source of variance. This of course left some notion of nation/ nationality as the source of any observed difference in values.

Reflecting upon the data collected, Hofstede (1980) first suggested that national business cultures vary according to four dimensions:

- Power distance

  For Hofstede, the concept of 'power distance' relates to the extent to which individuals are inclined to accept structural inequalities in power. Those countries with low 'power distance' scores, he argues, are egalitarian; they are disinclined to accept the centralization of decision-making and, consequently, prefer consultative over directive actions. Conversely, those countries with high power distance indices are said to be marked by obvious asymmetries which act to separate decision-makers from decision-takers.

- Individualism/collectivism

  Individualistic societies are said to diminish the social obligations and reciprocities that pertain in more collectivist settings. Hofstede suggests that individualist societies are bureaucratic yet prone to market fluctuations. Hofstede argues that collectivist societies, in contrast, are built upon the advantages enjoyed by 'in groups' which trade company loyalty for ongoing protection from the vagaries of the market.

- Masculinity/femininity

  This duality, Hofstede tells us, relates to the extent to which national cultures exhibit clearly defined gender roles. Masculine formations are said to exhibit clear gender divisions that require men to be assertive, tough, and focused upon material matters. Feminine cultures in contrast are said to be empathetic and focused upon the quality of relationships. Feminine cultures in contrast to masculine variants have gender roles that are looser and overlapping. Managers in feminine cultures are, as Hofstede suggests, expected to be intuitive and are expected to seek consensus and social solidarity.

- Uncertainty avoidance

  This aspect of national culture, Hofstede argues, addresses the extent to which cultural members feel threatened by uncertain or unfamiliar situations. Those cultures that struggle with uncertainty, Hofstede argues, compensate by focusing upon precision and punctuality. Indeed, he suggests that members of such cultures may engage in displacement activities, keeping busy to accommodate the stress of uncertainty. Cultures built upon the avoidance of uncertainty therefore are said to be constitutionally ill-suited to 'change'.

Later, Hofstede (1991) tells us that he chose to revise his dimensions when it became apparent that the uncertainty avoidance trait was, largely, irrelevant within the Chinese context. Thus, the uncertainty avoidance trait was downgraded from a general to a more localized trait, and 'Confucian dynamism' was added to offer a fuller appreciation of national cultures.

- Confucian dynamism

  Hofstede's concept of Confucian dynamism is an attempt to come to terms with the extent to which cultures take either a long-term or short-term view. Societies which take a long-term view, he tells us, grow and develop but do so in ways that are designed to build upon and to incorporate longer-standing traditions. More short-termist cultures are, in contrast, more cavalier with their heritage.

Later still, this time working with others (Hostede, Hofestede and Minkov, 2010), Hofstede added a sixth dimension to his model to address issues relating to the extent to which individuals are said to exercise restraint.

- Indulgence/restraint

  Indulgent cultures, as Hofstede suggests, are happy, optimistic about the future and protective of their right to freedom of expression. More restrained cultures he suggests are governed by stricter social norms that make social interaction controlled and regimented. Those from restrained cultural formations are, Hofstede argues, pessimistic.

Hofstede's work suggests that British business cultures are notable for being individualist, masculine, comfortable with uncertainty, and short term in their planning. Furthermore, he observes that British businesses tend to have a low power–distance ratio. In contrast, Scandinavian countries are said to exhibit more 'feminine' characteristics. Chinese and Taiwanese cultures, perhaps unsurprisingly given the labelling conventions adopted by Hofstede, are said to adopt long-term perspectives that honour and incorporate more traditional aspects of their societies.

Yet, not all are convinced by Hofstede's work. McSweeney (2002: 90), whose work is among the most cited of the critiques, observes that while Hofstede has added to his model over time 'he has never acknowledged any significant errors or weaknesses in [his] research'. McSweeney counters however that there *are* very significant errors and foundational weaknesses in the work of Hofstede. For example he points out that Hofstede seems to shift his position on the nature of national cultural differences.

At certain junctures, McSweeney observes, Hofstede seems to suggest that each of us will carry and embody the cultural traits said to be associated, uniquely, with our territorial borders. Yet for this assumption to hold, we must a) embrace 'national cultural determinism' (McSweeney, 2002: 92) and we must be prepared b) to overlook the manifold tensions that persist between 'nation' and 'state'. Am I for example a citizen of the United Kingdom, a British subject, or of Scotland?

Yet at other junctures, Hofstede seems to suggest that the national cultural traits represented within his work amount to central statistical tendency. In other words, Hofstede hedges on the nature and status of cultural traits; he fudges the issue and – as McSweeney learned – tends to play the man instead of the ball when challenged.

While risking the fury of Hofstede, therefore, we might ask: if national culture is common across the whole IBM estate and if culture is, indeed, the software of the mind, programming our responses to issues and problems, why is it that Hofstede offers an account of just 40 of the 66 territories?

At key points, as McSweeney observes, Hofstede has suggested that he could produce valid results from very small samples because he has been able to control for all other forms of variation other than nationality. McSweeney of course suggests that Hofstede's claims in this regard are utterly bogus, but if for a moment we indulge his voodoo statistics we might reasonably ask: what's the problem with the 26 territories excluded?

We could, while risking Hofstede's fury, take this critique further. Indeed as we shall see, some 40 years on from its original development, it may be useful to review Hofstede's analysis and the other models discussed in this thread as cultural artefacts in their own right. We will turn to this in our next thread.

Note

1 In fairness, we should point out that Lutz does, in fact, offer a geo-political reading of the US automobile industry and its travails.

5   Sexism, racism, and other common cultural practices

Introduction

In this section, we will offer a critical reading of 'organizational culture' and a review of the models discussed before. We embark upon this endeavour by first offering further reflections on the 'strong' and 'weak' cultures identified by Deal and Kennedy (1982). This constitution of cultures as variously strong(er) and weak(er), we will suggest, demonstrates the extent to which the models of culture prepared for students of management are, in themselves, cultural artefacts; perspectival projections of power and interest which must now be challenged and reviewed. To this end and calling upon the work of Schein (1985), we will suggest that the typologies of culture used to introduce students to what has become, apparently, the central concern of management are (at best) unconscious expressions of privilege, which suggest that full organizational membership is available only to a minority of the population.

Having revealed the cultural preferences and biases within the models discussed in our previous thread, we will attempt to secure a more inclusive account of culture. Challenging the assumption that culture is an organizational attribute, something which an organization 'has', we will suggest that the terms 'organization' and 'culture' are in effect synonyms. In short, we will argue that organizations 'are' cultures. Furthermore, we will argue that such cultures are altogether more complex, more fluid, more dynamic, and much more porous than the textbooks allow.

In the end and in an attempt to understand 'culture' from 'the native's perspective', we will consider the link between cultures and stories highlighted by Martin and her colleagues (1983). We will use this final element to jump across to our sixth thread which will, as our sub-title suggests, redeem the study of culture through an analysis of storytelling.

Reviewing culture

Deal and Kennedy, as we have seen, situate 'culture' as a response to 'risk' and market 'feedback'. This framework has become central to the management curriculum. It is something that all students are expected to know. Indeed, it is a model that students are expected to be able to reproduce and to discuss. And, to be fair, we should acknowledge that the headline analysis developed by Deal and Kennedy is plausible insofar as organizations do often exhibit different cultural priorities and concerns related to risk and feedback. Yet few students are, it seems to me, invited to engage critically with the frameworks developed, ostensibly, to explain and to account for organizational culture. In this thread, we will rethink 'culture' as this has been constituted within management studies.

Commenting on the work of Hofstede, McSweeney (2002) notes that critiques of (national) culture might be structured around concerns related, for example, to measurement and methodology. Recognizing this, I will nevertheless essay a different response. I will suggest that the typologies developed by Deal and Kennedy (1982), Handy ([1978] 2010), Schein (1985), and Hofstede (1980, 1991; Hofstede, Hofstede and Minkov, 2010) might be read as expressions of power and interest; as cultural artefacts in their own right insofar as they a) privilege a managerial or top-down perspective, and in so doing adopt b) a curious silence on those elements of our organized lives that any decent individual would surely question.

Reviewing Deal and Kennedy

As we have seen, Deal and Kennedy sub-divide their four cultural types into 'weak(er)' and 'strong(er)' variants. Strong cultures are those deemed to be amenable to managerial control and direction, whereas weaker forms are taken to be troublesome insofar as they resist this sort of intervention. This articulation of 'culture' is however deeply problematic. It is, for example, clear that the cultural behaviours which allowed employees to resist Taylor's 'scientific management', and to smooth out the economics of piece work, are only 'weak' and/or sub-optimal if we regard employees as culturally deficient children unschooled in the ways of the world. Yet, as we have demonstrated, workers employed within Taylorist systems of production have been obliged to develop (and to police) cohesive social formations, precisely, because they understand that the production systems imposed upon them by management are contrary to their needs and orientations. What Deal and Kennedy have constructed as 'weak cultures' therefore might now be understood as an empirical failure (a denial of evidence) that is, in fact, consequent upon the simplistic projection of managerial interests. In short, the 'weak' cultures belittled by Deal and Kennedy have this failing only insofar as we are prepared to assume that management 'knows best' and that the formations preferred at the strategic apex are truly 'strong', 'vibrant', and 'productive'. Yet Deal and Kennedy are not alone in allowing idealism to triumph over objectivism. As we shall see, Handy and Hofstede make similar choices and ironically Schein (1985) may help us to understand how and why.

Unconscious bias?

Schein (1985) suggests that cultures are layered. Echoing Hall's 'iceberg' metaphor, Schein suggests that most of culture is not directly observable and must be inferred from the study of artefacts and from the interpretation of visible behaviours. Indeed, he warns us that culture resides in 'the unconscious'. In other publications (see Collins, 1998, 2000, 2021b), I have disputed this construction. Calling upon the work of Feldman (1986), I have argued that Schein's work is deeply flawed, because in locating the very foundations of our cultural lives in 'the unconscious', Schein moves the analysis of 'culture' from the social realm to the psychologist's couch.

Noting the manner in which a focus upon 'the unconscious' acts to obfuscate the concepts and processes which merit more critical, analytical reflection, Feldman (1986: 87 original emphasis) complains that, despite its widespread use and application within the field of management, Schein's approach uses 'one of the most misunderstood concepts in the social sciences'. Thus, Feldman warns us that 'the term "unconscious" does not refer to a place, but is a linguistic device to *describe* not *locate* mental phenomena'. In short, Feldman suggests that Schein misunderstands the very essence of organizational culture! Yet Schein may offer some insight into the biases which have caused a bunch of privileged white males to constitute account of cultures which reflect and accommodate their own very comfortable lives.

You will recall that two of the four cultural types identified by Deal and Kennedy (1982) are defined, in turn, as 'tough guy, macho' and as 'work hard/play hard' cultures. And to be fair to the authors, there was much in US management, within this period, that was deserving of the macho epithet.

Discussing the career of Harold Geneen, the man who, between 1959 and 1977, transformed ITT from a US business into a multinational conglomerate with 350 businesses across 80 countries and who delivered 58 consecutive quarters of double-digit growth (see Geneen and Moscow, 1986), Pascale and Athos ([1981] 1986) offer us insights on the practice of management during this period. Indeed, the account of Geneen developed by Pascale and Athos, as we shall see, suggests that Deal and Kennedy are correct when they highlight *machismo* as a key part of US business culture:

> Harold Geneen has become one important archetype of the successful American manager. He was aggressive, competitive, forceful and downright threatening, hard and decisive. . . . That he remains such a respected figure and is often used to support arguments for similar behaviour is significant. Geneen represents in high relief a modern version of a historical approach to management. He is Mr. Theory X, if you will. And for many executives just calling him to mind is satisfying. *Imagine* having that much power, control, intellectual ability, skill and getting those bottom-line results.
>
> (Pascale and Athos ([1981] 1986: 151 original emphasis)

Yet, even Geneen recognized a downside to *machismo*. Highlighting the manner in which a 'work hard, play hard' culture exacts a price from those subject to its demands, Geneen (Geneen and Moscow, 1986) draws attention to the 'in-house alcoholics treatment and referral programme' (129) that ITT was obliged to establish in 1973. He reports that 6500 employees and family members received assistance from this programme between 1975 and 1985.

Geneen's world is, of course, a *macho* world. It is also, we should note, plainly and in any sense 'a man's world'. Indeed, we should observe that in his text on 'managing', Geneen simply presumes that managers *are* men and hence uses the male pronoun throughout. Yet, there is one exception to this pattern. When Geneen discusses alcoholism women suddenly make an appearance in his narrative: 'I am told that in recent years 89% of men and women referred to the programme have been rehabilitated and retained in their jobs rather than fired' (129).

That bullying is condoned and that women appear in this narrative of 'managing' only as a source of corporeal breakdown and organizational disorder is, I think, instructive! It suggests to me that far from representing a simple inventory of structures, policies, and artefacts the typologies of culture developed to educate students and to inform managerial action must now be read as specific orderings of the social world, value-laden texts that like any other cultural artefact tells us something about the values, attitudes, and beliefs of the authors!

Recognizing this, we might now inquire:

• Were the braying, arrogant men (and they are typically men) who populate the 'macho' cultural formation really role models worthy of note and celebration in the 1980s? And in 2021 should we even allow such fools a voice at all?

- Why is it that Deal and Kennedy seem prepared to overlook the macho misogynistic excesses of these social formations? As tutors, we would round upon any student who dared to suggest that the display of pornographic images in the workplace is alright; *just one of those things*; boys . . . you know! But we are content, it seems, to relay without comment or further reflection models that happily indulge all manner of misogyny in the name of 'business needs'!

Equally, we might ask:

- Why is it that Deal and Kennedy seem to look down upon 'process cultures'? Why are these represented as economic backwaters – rest homes for those neurotics who, because they suffer this affliction, seem, somehow, undeserving of the rewards associated with full organizational membership?
- Is it coincidence that the organizations said to display the attributes of a 'process culture' are those that employ predominantly women?

We may raise similar concerns in connection with Handy's (1985) typology.

Reviewing Handy

Handy (1985), as we have seen, suggests that organizations may be divided into:

- Power cultures – where all decisions and all forms of communication are channelled through a single individual or organizational node.
- Role cultures – where decisions are made by more-or-less complex bureaucracies populated by individuals selected for the knowledge acquired through education and on-the-job training.
- Task cultures – which in contrast to the bureaucratic organizing principles of the role culture appear to be organized on an *ad hoc* basis.
- Person cultures – which might be considered to be loose coalitions of individuals and organizations in name only.

In common with the typology proffered by Deal and Kennedy (1982), Handy's account of cultural types is, at one level, plausible. Concrete examples of each type come readily to mind and were suggested in our fourth thread. Benedict ([1934] 1989: 238) of course has warned us that what appears to be 'a type' of culture, 'a fixed constellation of traits', is more usefully constituted as 'a pattern', an 'empirical characterization . . . not duplicated in its entirety anywhere else in the world'. Yet, since Handy's model is routinely deployed in teaching to offer students and practitioners (ostensibly) an appreciation of cultural values and organizational dynamics, we might reasonably ask:

- Why does Handy acknowledge Benedict's influence and yet insist on treating 'culture' as a type rather than as a pattern?
- Why does Handy suggest that the boorish and bullying culture of the 'power culture' is a business problem that limits the ability of 'the culture' to develop and to reproduce when it might have been couched as an ethical issue?

In a similar vein, we might ask questions designed to reveal the cultural preferences, priorities, and, indeed, prejudices within what seem to be simple descriptions of national culture. For example:

- Why is it that Hofstede's (1980) account of cultural traits adopts an anti-union position? Why, given the work of Freeman and Medoff (1984), which demonstrates that unions bring benefits to groups otherwise notable for being marginal in economic terms, does Hofstede feel at liberty to suggest that trades unions are monopoly providers of labour who secure benefits for their members by excluding outsiders?
- And why do so many of those who employ Hofstede's work (critically or otherwise) in their teaching fail to highlight this projection?

Similarly, we might ask:

- Why does Hofstede choose to frame risk-taking, decisiveness, and assertiveness as male traits?
- Indeed, in the year 2021, how are women, and for that matter members of the BAME and LGBTQ+ communities, supposed to read models of organizational culture that are predominantly male and very obviously white and heterosexual? Is 'don't ask, don't tell' still the preferred policy when it come to the management of diversity?

Surely a management education fit for the second decade of the twenty-first century should have something to say about race, gender, and identity. Indeed would not a 'liberal' education 'call out' sexism, racism, and homophobia and in so doing offer strategies, both individual and organizational, designed to address these concerns?

In an attempt to provide the analytical tools necessary for an alternative pedagogy on culture, we will now turn our attention to the division evident between those who suggest that organizations 'have' cultures and those who insist that organizations 'are' cultures.

Do organizations have cultures?

The models of culture reviewed here and, indeed, the majority of texts prepared for students plainly regard culture as a variable that managers may choose to alter, once they have come to terms with its core components. Yet in making the suggestion that culture may be manipulated, redirected, and changed from the top-down, the models reviewed in this thread and in the previous thread tend either to assert, or to assume, that organizations 'have' cultures. Yet to suggest that organizations 'have' cultures is, surely, to allow space for the suggestion that some organized settings may simply lack cultures. Ogbonna and Wilkinson (1988) suggest as much in their analysis of a supermarket. Noting that supermarkets, often, suffer from high levels of staff turnover, the authors suggest that it may be easy to engineer cultural change within these settings because these organizations *don't really have cultures*.

Frankly, I scoff at this suggestion. Indeed I wonder if my colleagues travel the earth with their eyes closed because wherever I turn, I am confronted by very temporary forms of social organization which demonstrate some level of agreement on norms, values, and beliefs. Until quite recently, for example, Britons were required, by law, to form themselves into orderly queues when waiting for a bus. This law is no longer in force and outside London it is, I think, now rare to see orderly queues at bus stops. Instead, those wishing to take the bus in Norwich and Hull (to offer but two examples) tend to loiter around the bus stop in an apparently haphazard fashion. I say, apparently, because it is clear to me that those awaiting the bus are, on arrival at the stop, careful to note those present and in so doing form an orderly queue *in their minds*. When the bus arrives it is, frankly, wonderful to watch the controlled and orderly manner in which strangers, who may never see one another again, climb aboard the bus!

To me, this very temporary social organization exhibits 'culture': there is a shared *belief* (evidenced through conduct) which demonstrates that those present accept and abide by a core principle: that passengers *should* board the bus in the order at which they arrived at the stop. There is furthermore evidence of social norms. Thus my experience suggests that fairness is enforced (sort of) such that when someone breaches the boarding convention, they will be challenged in a very British fashion – by an audible 'tut' and an accompanying frosty stare.

If a group of people gathered for only a few minutes at a bus stop can secure and enact what amounts to a common cultural understanding, it seems to me ludicrous to assert that a supermarket (or indeed any other social setting) would somehow lack a culture. As the film *Pirates of the Caribbean* reminds us even cut-throats live by 'a code'. Indeed it is, perhaps, worth observing that this film adopts a very playful position as regards the status and operation of 'the pirate code' which usefully illustrates, I suggest, the manner in which each of us tends to interpret and in so doing to renegotiate the cultural prescriptions that Hofstede (1991) and Atkinson (1997) assert act as mental programs which control our behaviour. Thus it is worth observing that at key points within the film *Pirates of the Caribbean* – where adherence to 'the pirate code' would make life difficult, dangerous, or inconvenient for our key protagonists – this code is quickly downgraded to 'a set of guidelines'!

Putting this perhaps more formally: if an organizational setting cannot be conceived in the absence of 'culture', this necessarily implies that culture is properly understood as the very essence of social organization. In short, my musings on bus queues, pirates, and supermarkets demonstrate that organizations do not have cultures they *are* cultures!

This recognition of organizations-as-cultures is very clearly advanced by Ackroyd and Crowdy (1990). Offering an ethnographic study of a group of slaughterhouse workers, the authors suggest that to understand and to express the core dynamics of social organization, we must accept that organizations *are* cultures. Indeed, they demonstrate that organizations are cultural formations that will tend to object to, and in so doing, will tend to out-pace attempts to impose top-down management control and/or change.

Ackroyd and Crowdy, we should note, acknowledge that the culture of the slaughterhouse workers they observed is pretty macho. Indeed this group is, we should note, expected to work hard and to play hard. Yet unlike Deal and Kennedy, Ackroyd and Crowdy do not celebrate this. They are clear that this work group is governed by fear and physical intimidation. And for this and other reasons, Ackroyd and Crowdy find the slaughterhouse workers to be vain and pitiful creatures. Elaborating upon this portrayal, the authors point out that the work that these men undertake – they kill and render animals – makes it difficult for them to circulate in polite society. The question *And what do you do?* becomes a recurrent nightmare for the slaughter men just as the members of polite society recoil in horror at the fact of their employment.

The slaughterhouse men, we should observe, claim to take pride in their work. Few men, they suggest, would have the stomach for this sort of work, which is undoubtedly true. And yet at the same time, it is clear that despite their protestations, the slaughterhouse workers are shamed by what they do for a living, because they scarcely interact with the community beyond the broader environs of the slaughterhouse.

Reflecting upon the manner in which this social isolation shapes the culture of the slaughterhouse, Ackroyd and Crowdy note that it is extraordinarily cohesive. Yet this formation is quite unlike the conventional 'work hard/ play hard culture', identified by Deal and Kennedy (1982). Indeed the authors observe that the slaughterhouse workers represent a powerful counter-culture that successfully opposes even the most rudimentary demands of management.

And what is it that makes this counter-culture so powerful? It is the fact that the social ties of this grouping extend beyond the workplace into the ties of friendship and kinship. This recognition of the manner in which hearth and home shapes (and is shaped by) the culture of the workplace should serve to remind us of something that the models reviewed before tend to ignore, namely that workplaces are located within overlapping cultural formations – family, school, community, church etc. – that may question the legitimacy of the demands made by management. This recognition of 'cultural porosity' suggests that organizational cultures are much more complex and much more interconnected than we have been led to believe. Indeed, the work of Ackroyd and Crowdy reminds us that some workplace cultures (like that of the slaughter men) may all but confound the polite sensibilities of senior management and will be, consequently, nigh on impossible to manage let alone change. Martin (1992), as we shall see, offers a framework that captures this complexity rather well.

Three perspectives on culture

Martin (1992) offers three contrasting perspectives on culture.

*   An integration perspective
*   A differentiation perspective
*   A fragmentation perspective

Martin observes that while most management commentators tend to proceed from an 'integration' perspective, which suggests that organizational cultures are united and cohesive, there are legitimate challenges to this position. For example she suggests an alternative 'differentiation' perspective which views the organization in pluralistic terms as being composed of a range of (more-or-less) supportive sub-cultures that may be prepared to work together in order to secure a useful consensus position on (for example) the organization's core structure and purpose. Yet, this differentiation perspective does not exhaust the possibilities discussed by Martin.

Indeed, the fragmentation perspective on culture invites us to consider counter-cultural formations that have grown up to dispute the competence and/or the legitimacy of the managerial elite. It is worth observing, however, that 'fragmented' cultures may continue to be highly productive. Thus, the workplace described by Ackroyd and Crowdy, to return to our earlier example, is notable for being highly productive in the absence of detailed management control and direction!

You may have observed that in a passage given earlier, I made reference to 'uncovering' social phenomena. I do enjoy a rhetorical flourish, of course, but I have chosen this term very carefully because if our reflections on the constitution of culture have taught us anything it is, surely, that we must be careful to challenge and to reveal, uncover, and overturn the presumptions which continue to distort our understanding of organizations-as-cultures, where necessary. Working with colleagues, Joanne Martin (Martin et al., 1983) offers reflections on storytelling which, because they provide a useful counterpoint to top-down accounts of culture and change (Collins, 2013), offer us resources that might uncover and in so doing overturn the presumptions that shape our understanding of organizational culture and cultural change.

The uniqueness paradox

Martin et al. (1983: 439) observe that most organizational cultures make a claim to uniqueness. They observe, too, that when challenged, organizational members generally seek to substantiate this claim to uniqueness by referencing cultural manifestations such as stories. Yet Martin and her colleagues point out that the organizational stories, which they have encountered through their research, 'exhibit a remarkable similarity in content and structure'. There exists therefore a 'uniqueness paradox' in the sense that '*a culture's claim to uniqueness is expressed through cultural manifestations that are not in fact unique*' (439 original emphasis).

Examining organizational stories as cultural manifestations, Martin et al. argue that 'seven stories that make tacit claims to uniqueness . . . occur, in virtually identical form, in a wide variety of organizations' (439).

To aid analysis of these seven story-types, the authors identify the tales as a series of questions which, in highlighting core anxieties in relation to the experience of work, narrate the organization 'from below':

1   Do senior organizational members abide by the rules that they have set down?
2   Is the big boss human?
3   Is the organization meritocratic?

4   Will I get fired?
5   Will the organization assist me to relocate?
6   How does the organization deal with mistakes?
7   How does the organization deal with obstacles?

These seven story forms, while not exhaustive of narrative possibilities, are, the authors argue, widespread *and* enduring because they 'express tensions that arise from a conflict between organizational exigencies and the values of employees, which are, in turn reflective of the values of the larger society' (447). Indeed, Martin et al. suggest that the story-types which arise in relation to the anxieties expressed in the questions given before circulate widely and are maintained within the memory of organizations because they project deep-seated concerns which organizational members have with respect to:

•   Equality
•   Security
•   Control

Reviewing the relationship between these core anxieties and the seven story-types identified in and through their research, Martin and her colleagues argue that the stories developed in response to questions 1, 2, and 3 (as given before) deal with concerns related to equality and inequality at work. Stories developed in response to questions 4, 5, and 6, in contrast, relate to tensions formed around a security–insecurity duality. In the end, stories developed in response to question 7 reflect concerns with respect to control and autonomy in this context.

The work of Martin and her colleagues was published around the same time as the models of culture reviewed before. Yet unlike these models, the work of Martin and her colleagues reveals aspects of organization that have, in effect, been written out of the analysis of 'organizational culture'. Indeed, the shared tales revealed by Martin and her co-authors suggest that the models of culture prepared for students of management lack authenticity; they deny social organization as a lived experience because they privilege an elite perspective that simply fails to give 'the native' – the insider at the bottom of the pyramid – a voice.

In our next thread, we will suggest that stories possess the capacity to redeem the analysis of organizational culture . . . if we are prepared to find and/or develop tales that embrace the lived complexities of social organization that make cultures dynamic.

6 Redeeming organizational culture

Stories and storytelling

Introduction

Writing some decades ago, the sociologist C. Wright-Mills (1973) offered a critical reading of academic sociology. The processes designed to make academic work reliable and hence reproducible, he argued, had secured rigor at the cost of authenticity and had converted the subjects of sociological analysis into objects to be manipulated by researchers. Famously, he suggested that those who would know of the affairs of men and women should abandon the study of sociology and should, instead, immerse themselves in novels. Explaining this radical strategy, Wright-Mills argued that novelists had continued to develop very human accounts of the trials, triumphs, and tribulations of our mundane lives even as the sociologists abandoned their subjects.

In this thread, I will throw my weight behind this suggestion. I will argue that organizational stories, because they retain the capacity to constitute the organization from the bottom-up, have the ability to reconfigure our appreciation of organization-as-cultures. In this thread, therefore, I will offer reflections on stories and storytelling designed to redeem the analysis of organizations-as-cultures.

I will begin by offering a brief account of the essence of the poetic tale as rendered by Gabriel (2000). Gabriel's work, as we shall see, is preoccupied with the stories that circulate (orally) within organizations. This focus, as we shall see, causes Gabriel to reflect upon tales which are reasonably short and which build upon fairly simple plotting devices. While accepting and endorsing, Gabriel's approach – truthfully the work of Gabriel has shaped much of my own work in this arena – I will extend his account of storytelling to accommodate the work of Booker (2007). Where Gabriel focuses upon the spoken word – stories as lived and shared experience – Booker is more concerned with the novel. The tales reviewed by Booker are, consequently, bigger and more complex, and this, as we shall see, is reflected in the manner in which he catalogues and accounts for the stories we share.

Building upon the devices developed by Gabriel and by Booker, I will offer suggestions for reading and reflection designed to demonstrate ways in which an interest in storytelling might be used to redeem organizational culture to develop more rounded and more authentic accounts of culture that can provide a more solid basis for managerial reflection and action.

The essence of stories

Gabriel (2000) notes that academia has tended to treat stories as quaint subordinates to fact. In recent years, however, this position has, he tells us, been called into question by scholars inclined to a more qualitative form of analysis. Rejecting the proscriptions of positivism, Gabriel argues that stories are not, simply, pre-modern artefacts that now require protection and preservation. They are instead vital constituents of social organization, which explain and account for who we are.

Weick (1995) endorses this position. He argues that storytelling is a response to ambiguity. We tell tales to ourselves and others, he warns us, so that we might filter and reduce the noise that is our daily life. In this respect, stories are enacted as 'the signal' – they animate and orientate. And they are, Weick argues, driven by plausibility rather than by accuracy.

Gabriel reminds us, however, that we must exercise some discipline in the analysis of storytelling. Stories are, he insists, special forms of narrative which possess core structural characteristics. These characteristics, he warns us, differentiate 'stories' from related narratives forms such as 'opinions', 'proto-stories', and 'reports'.

- 'Opinions'

These narratives, Gabriel argues, may contain factual or symbolic materials. However, Gabriel's analysis suggests that these narratives seek to 'tell' rather than to 'show' the audience what has happened. Consequently, 'opinions' may lack the seductive qualities necessary to convince others that the events under scrutiny are fully relevant to their concerns or consonant with their experience.

- 'Proto-stories'

These narratives may have a rudimentary plot device and some level of characterization. Yet they remain incomplete insofar as they offer, for example, a beginning and middle but no satisfactory ending.

- 'Reports'

These narratives, Gabriel argues, offer an historic rather than a poetic rendering of events and so produce stubbornly factually and causative, as opposed to symbolic, accounts. Reports, therefore, are monological. They invite factual verification and so seek to crystallize events as an empirical reality.

- 'Stories'

Stories are local, organic, and essentially polyphonic in character. They:

- involve characters in a predicament;
- unfold according to a chain of events that reflects a) the structure of the plot and b) the essential traits of the characters involved;
- call upon symbolism/symbolic matters;
- indulge poetic embellishment and narrative development'
- have an arc which moves the reader/ audience from a beginning through a middle section to a successful conclusion; and
- seek a connection not with simple facts but with local understandings and/or more general truths.

The '6Fs' of narratives

The recognition that stories depend upon poetic license and indulge embellishment suggests that storytellers must work to enrol their readers in a common project. Dickens ([1841] 1922) captures this important aspect of the storyteller's art. As he introduces *A Christmas Carol*, Dickens takes special care to warn his readers that the success of his tale will depend upon their commitment to, and their collusion in, the exercise of a form of poetic licence that can conjure the dead. Thus, Dickens begins his classic tale with the following observations and questions:

> Marley was dead: to begin with. There is no doubt whatever about that. The register of his burial was signed by the clergyman, the clerk, the undertaker, and the chief mourner. Scrooge signed it: and Scrooge's name was good upon 'Change for anything he chose to put his hand to. Old Marley was dead as a door-nail.
>
> Mind! I don't mean to say that I know, of my own knowledge, what there is particularly dead about a door-nail. I might have been inclined, myself, to regard a coffin-nail as the deadest piece of ironmongery in the trade. But the wisdom of our ancestors is in the simile; and my unhallowed hands shall not disturb it, or the Country's done for. You will therefore permit me to repeat, emphatically, that Marley was dead as a door-nail.
>
> Scrooge knew he was dead? Of course he did. How could it be otherwise? Scrooge and he were partners for I don't know how many years. Scrooge was his sole executor, his sole administrator, his sole assign,

his sole residuary legatee, his sole friend and sole mourner. And even Scrooge was not so dreadfully cut up by the sad event, but that he was an excellent man of business on the very day of the funeral, and solemnized it with an undoubted bargain.

The mention of Marley's funeral brings me back to the point I started from. There is no doubt that Marley was dead. This must be distinctly understood, or nothing wonderful can come of the story I am going to relate.

(Dickens, [1841] 1922: 1–3)

This distinction between stories and reports, while somewhat strained in practice (see Collins, 2018, 2021b; Collins and Rainwater, 2005), reminds us that whereas reporters chronicle the world, storytellers must be allowed, where necessary, to rearrange characters, situations, and events in order to secure a) the attention and b) the ongoing affiliation of their audiences. Pursuing this distinction between stories and reports, Gabriel (2004) tells us that the practice of storytelling will call upon '6F' factors. Namely:

Framing

Where characters are arranged as being, variously, central or marginal to the tale.

Focusing

Where special emphasis is placed upon a particular cluster of events and/or characters at the expense of other movements and actors.

Filtering

Where certain events or characters are removed from a tale in order to secure the integrity of the plot-line or to maintain the pace of the story.

Fading

Where specific events or characters are introduced or/then removed from the tale to reflect the needs of the plot.

Fusing

Where multiple events and/or characters are merged into singularities to collapse, for example, temporal distinctions.

Fitting

Where characters or events are reinterpreted or represented in line with the overall requirements of the story as opposed to, say, the actual historical records of events.

The artful arrangement of these structural components, Gabriel notes, allows storytellers to develop:

- 'epic',
- 'comic',
- 'romantic', and
- 'tragic' story forms.

The epic story-type circulates widely in many published accounts of organization and management. In this managerial context, 'epic' tales concern the lives and endeavours of those who have, variously, led, changed, and/or 'saved' organizations (see Collins and Rainwater, 2005). Epic tales often have simple and rather linear plot-lines. Indeed, epic tales tend to devote little time to the intricacies and complexities of character development. Instead they focus upon action, movement, achievement, and closure.

In more classical renderings of the story-types discussed by Gabriel, comic tales are those that conclude with an improvement in the fortunes of the central character. In Gabriel's schema, however, this is adjusted to reflect, I suggest, the realities of the organizational settings that shape his concerns. For Gabriel, therefore, comic tales are designed to produce laughter.

The 'tragic' tale in contrast is defined by its tendency to visit a reversal of fortunes on the main character. Thus, where the 'epic' tale is said to invite us to admire and to celebrate the deeds of its central character, 'tragic' tales induce feelings of loss and pity.

The 'romantic' form as you might expect deals, broadly, with love and with affairs of the heart. Gabriel observes that this story-form is rarely uncovered within organizations by researchers. Commenting on this finding, Gabriel suggests that this outcome may reflect a cultural assumption that such matters are inappropriate and unwelcome within an environment, framed publicly by serious and rational decision-making. Offering an auxiliary hypothesis to explain the absence of the romantic form in organizational contexts, Gabriel suggests that romantic tales are seldom unearthed in workplace research because those engaged in storytelling research fail to develop the rapport necessary to allow respondents to render such tales with confidence in settings that tend to deny legitimacy to such feelings.

Deal and Kennedy (1982) and other advocates of/for 'popular management' (see Collins, 2018) have, of course, highlighted the extent to which stories signal cultural values. Furthermore, they have suggested that managers *should* craft stories to signal new priorities and to demonstrate the desirable forms of behaviour required within the organization's culture. This is, of course, a plausible line of argument. Stories do tend to signal priorities and they do have a capacity to animate and to orientate us . . . but only, I suggest, if we can find or create authentic tales that a) connect with cultural norms and values while b) signalling opportunities for change that are sensitive to context and history. Alas, the tales developed and curated within organizations to achieve this outcome tend to lack authenticity.

Collins (2007), for example, suggests that the tales which managers develop and share are based, typically, upon epic narratives. These narratives, he complains, are shrill, one-dimensional, and focused upon top-down concerns (see Collins, 2021b). Reflecting upon the patterns of inclusion and exclusion evident in the work of a leading management commentator, Collins (2012) argues that tales of organization designed to signal culture change too often suggest that women cannot achieve and indeed do not deserve full membership of the organization's culture. Furthermore, Collins (2013) suggests that the tales developed by Tom Peters simply fail to acknowledge the anxieties that arise in connection with insecurity in the workplace.

We will return to these issues as we offer stories designed to reveal and to redeem 'culture', but for the moment we must pause to consider Booker's (2007) analysis of storytelling.

The heartbeat of the story

Gabriel (2000) suggests that stories are, in any sense, vital components of social organization. The stories we craft, the stories we recall, and the stories we tell one another quite literally shape our worlds and ourselves. Booker (2007), I suggest, would probably accept this; yet his focus is different because he is concerned with stories-as-literature. This shift from stories-as-spoken to stories-as-written and stories-as-read obliges Booker to develop a broader catalogue of tales that can embrace the richness of 'the novel'.

In common with Gabriel, Booker (2007) embraces an Aristotelian (1965) account of the essence of the poetic tale. He refines this position, however, and suggests that each story arc will move through five phases, developing as it does what amounts to 'a heartbeat' involving two phases of compression-release. The five stages of the tragedy, for example, Booker names as:

1   The anticipation stage
2   The dream stage

Redeeming organizational culture 61

3   The frustration stage
4   The nightmare stage
5   The destruction/death wish stage

In the anticipation stage of the tale, the hero is revealed as being some-how incomplete, lacking in fulfilment. As the opening, anticipation stage of the tale is developed, our hero receives a call to action which in provid-ing focus reveals his/her true purpose. Classic tragedies, Booker suggests, would include the tales of Macbeth and Icarus. However, a contemporary example might include that of the disgraced cyclist, Lance Armstrong (see Walsh, 2013; Macur, 2014).

In the dream stage of the tale there is, often, a brief period when all goes well for our tragic hero. Booker suggests that, at this stage, the distinction between the tragedy and more positive plots turns upon the hero's response to the call to action received in the first stage. In epic or quest-type sto-ries, for example, Booker suggests that the hero responds quickly to the call, and the reader is assured that this is, definitively, the correct course of action. In tragic plots, however, our hero hesitates. This hesitation and the fact that the hero of the tragedy chooses to hide his final commitment to the call to action, Booker suggests, demonstrates that our hero has yielded to a temptation that will surely provoke his/her final destruction. In the story of *Dr. Jekyll and Mr. Hyde*, for example, we know that Jekyll is doing wrong because he conducts his experiments in secret. Indeed, we understand that he keeps these experiments from his wife and from his colleagues because he knows that he is embarking on a project that is, both, dangerous and inappropriate.

We can see similarities in Armstrong's case. For example we can see that in choosing to dope so that he might prosper within a sporting arena, defined by drug-taking and blood-supplements, Armstrong embarked upon a path that will see him increasingly cut off from the community that, inno-cently and naively, celebrates his achievements. In the opening phases of, what will soon reveal itself to be a tragedy, however, Armstrong prospers. He wins major titles, gathers wealth, and is publicly applauded.

Taken together, the anticipation and dream stages provide the first compression-release cycle suggested by Booker. But this is the opening phase of the tale, and for Armstrong the tragedy is soon to be revealed.

In the frustration stage our hero, having responded to his/her call and having experienced rewards and fulfilment through so doing, now experi-ences new frustrations. Our hero is once again denied peace and rest. His/her world is – figuratively at least – subject to a new compression.

In the nightmare stage, the pressures which were built once more during the frustration stage are resolved as the tragic hero loses control of his/her world. In the Armstrong tale, this second compression-release cycle might be structured around a number of Gabriel's 'F' devices. If, for example, we conclude the dream stage with Armstrong's retirement from competitive cycling, then we may commence the frustration stage with an account of the shadow that crept over his life.

Sitting at home on his sofa with a beer in his hand, Armstrong, it seems, finds that he simply cannot deal with the success of (lesser) rivals who, in his absence, have secured major titles, wealth, and respect. The choices made in this frustration stage, of course, lead inevitably to the nightmare stage where on his return to the sport, Armstrong endures accidents and crashes and while being bested on the road, becomes trapped by former colleagues who, having been used and abused by their former team leader, choose to assist those who have become convinced that Armstrong is a liar, cheat, and bully who must be held to account.

In the destruction/death-wish stage, our hero's true character is revealed, and as a consequence s/he is rejected by the community and ultimately destroyed. This destruction, Booker suggests, provides balance to a community that has been divided by the conduct of the central protagonist. In Armstrong's case, this revelation and rejection is secured on prime-time television as Oprah Winfrey demands answers to a series of yes/no questions which, as they reveal Armstrong to be a liar, cheat, and bully, rain down destruction upon his business empire and upon the self-image that he has built.

It has been suggested that the difference between tragedy and comedy often turns upon small details – upon the simple passage of time for example. This aphorism is of course basically true. Commenting upon the small differences that shape and define his 'basic plots', Booker reminds us of the small changes that can convert, for example, a tragedy into a comedy. Indeed, he suggests that in a schematic sense, the true difference between the tragic plot and the comic plot turns upon the final stage or movement. Thus, where the tragic tale culminates in a destructive phase that sees the community united in its cathartic pursuit of the disgraced hero, 'the comedy' turns upon a revelation that will see the hero and the community reunited as one. Similarly, we might observe that the tale of 'voyage and return' differs from the tragic schematic only in the final movement where the hero 'escapes and returns' to an earlier location/and or pattern of life.

The seven basic plots

Gabriel, as we have seen, suggests four main story-types; Booker, however, suggests that there are, in fact, seven basic plots that are endlessly repeated. These plots he labels as:

1 Overcoming the Monster

Tales of this form would include, for example, *Dracula, Frankenstein*, and *Jaws*, which see monsters, in a variety of forms, vanquished and the commonwealth secured.

2 Rags to Riches

Tales in this vein might include *The Wolf of Wall Street* and, perhaps, more positively *A Christmas Carol*.

3 Voyage and Return

Booker notes that there are obvious overlaps and parallels between his plot-types. For example, it is clear that a case could be made for the inclusion of *Jaws* within this category – or at least the second, ship-borne component of this story. That said, examples that clearly qualify within this category would include *The Odyssey* and the tale of *Orpheus*.

4 Comedy

Booker suggests that the comic plot is the most complex, contrived, and dynamic of the elemental plots. Yet he tells us that, at root, the plot of the comedy turns and depends upon the development of a revelation that provides reunification.

5 Tragedy

The tragedy is, in contrast, notable for the manner in which the plot-line first divides the community before securing reunification through the destruction of the tragic hero.

6 Rebirth

Tales of rebirth see our hero take a journey – literally or figuratively – that precipitates a fundamental reassessment of life choices. Within these tales, there is often, Booker suggests, a redeeming figure whose presence (and peril) precipitates change in the hero. Viewed from this perspective, *A Christmas Carol* might be considered a tale of rebirth *if* we are prepared to offer greater prominence to the character of Tiny Tim.

7 Dark Power

In plots concerning what Booker terms the dark power, we often encounter young people who have ventured, naively, into the world and are, as a consequence of their naïveté, open to the influence of 'dark powers'. Initially as in, for example, the tale of *Pinocchio*, the pleasures available to the holders of the dark power bring satisfaction to our hero; yet, as we end the first of the two compression-release cycles suggested by Booker (2007), we begin to encounter problems and frustrations and after a time the hero realizes that s/he has taken the wrong path in life and now faces a dreadful future. Positive versions of this form allow our hero an escape (Pinocchio escapes just before being condemned to life as an ass), whereas the alternative, negative form visits enduring loss and punishment upon the central figure.

Reflecting upon tales such as those that have been so carefully classified by Booker, Wright-Mills (1973) suggests that our novelists are skilled observers of the human condition. Noting that novelists probe and reveal the frailties, vanities, and prejudices of the human character, which have been written out of academic sociology and – for our purposes – the study of 'organizational culture', Wright-Mills suggests that those who would know of the dynamics of social organization should use novels to uncover and to call out the limitations of those typologies which claim to explain how people think feel and act at work.

A careful reading of novels, I suggest, will help to reveal and to acknowledge the dynamics of social organization and the divisions ignored and yet cemented within the academic study of organizational culture. In the remainder of this thread, therefore, I will offer reflections on a few texts, which I suggest, might be reviewed and employed to redeem our understanding of the many different ways in which people think, feel, and act (within) and about social organization. In the remainder of this thread, therefore, I will offer but a few texts (some of) which I enjoy and which I suggest might allow us to come to a renewed appreciation of the manners and more of social organization.

In the light of my earlier comments concerning the boorish conduct enabled by the typologies of culture which we teach students, it may be helpful to point out that the texts I will discuss are not, in any sense, oases of decency and/or 'political correctness'. I do not want to offer an account of 'culture-as-it-should be'; this is, after all, what 'popular management' provides albeit from the perspective of an elite. Instead I hope to offer an account of 'culture' that truly reflects experience beyond the elite. In short, my aim is to show, in relief, that within and between the organograms, mission statements, and value propositions, the workplace remains a social realm that is sectional, irrational, flawed, and laughable in so, so many ways.

In pursuit of this, I will use the fruits of 'creative writing' to invite the consideration of:

- The organizationally prosaic
- Organized profanity
- Organizational polyphony.

The prosaic

Deal and Kennedy (1982) focus upon the key symbols of organizational life and in keeping with the analysis developed by Peters and Waterman (1982) and by Kanter (1989) suggest that business leaders should develop and channel these, converting them into celebrations, rituals . . . *hoop-la!*

Yet, what none of these contributions to organization (and change) address is 'routine'; the mundane and the prosaic. In this section, I will draw upon one novel in particular to show the manner in which the daily grind – the slow procession of the hour hand – shapes thought and action in ways that are, it seems to me, simply lost on the elites who until now have been allowed to decide what matters to and for us.

Introducing *The Chatto Book of Office Life*, Jeremy Lewis (1992: 3–4) concedes that

> the fearful truth is that, however much office workers may rant and rage, office life is, for most of us, a matter of love as well as hate. Even the dullest of offices has an intrinsic fascination for those who work there, both in terms of the work itself and, even more importantly, in social terms: for like a rock pool of the underside of a stone, the office teems with unsuspected life. . . . Not surprisingly, given the amount of time we spend in these curious places, the friendships and the gossip and the intrigues and even the passions of office life may well loom larger than those of domestic life. Office life – like life in general – is often tedious and frightening and baffling, conducive to ulcers and nervous sweat and terrible sleepless nights, filled with dread of what the morning will bring, or a miserable awareness of life seeping away, almost unremarked. We dream of escape, of shaking off the yoke. . . . As for the ultimate dream of retirement . . . it's no surprise to learn that, deprived of routine, status and companionship all at once so many office workers peg out within months of receiving their retirement clock.

Taking our cue from Lewis, it seems sensible to begin this brief consideration of the rhythms and processes of working life – present in a shadowy form, but largely ignored by accounts of culture and change – with reflections on our performance within the routine that is necessary to secure entry to the first contact with that queer thing that is 'the workplace'.

Keith Waterhouse (1978: 27) offers useful insights on this ritual and on the manner in which the interviewee must quickly guess the response that will be culturally appropriate:

> Gryce sensed that this time Lucas was definitely asking a leading question, albeit an excessively fanciful one. An answer in the order of 'Oh

good heavens, no!' seemed to be called for. He plumped for this line but decided to embellish it a little.

'Oh good heavens, no! I've always found that whatever job I'm doing is in itself an end product. That is, you do what's required of you to the best of your ability, and someone else picks up his own process from there'.

Lucas appeared well satisfied. Gryce was glad, on balance, that he had not over-egged the pudding, by adding, 'No man could ask for more'.

'I'm pleased you said that. It's really just the attitude we're looking for as regards this particular vacancy. It's an in-house post as you know, Stationery Supplies, serving all the other departments in the building, and a certain type of personality might feel cut off from the mainstream. Far from the madding crowd'.

'Oh good heavens, no!' The job was his. It was in the bag.

It may be useful to meet this 'madding crowd'; to consider the manner in which the newcomer navigates it and in so doing ingratiates himself:

'Mr Graph-paper, Mr Seeds, Miss Divorce, Mrs Rashman, Mr Ad Dah, Mr Charles Penny, Mr New Penny, Mr Hakim'

Catching one name in three, Clement Gryce shook hands with such of his new colleagues as were near enough to touch, and nodded to those who were out of reach behind their desks.

Most of them said a word or two: 'How d'y'do'. 'Glad to have you aboard." 'Welcome to the madhouse'. They seemed a nice enough lot taken all round, though Gryce put question marks over the heads of two of them, Beastly and Graph-paper, who could very easily have shaken hands if they'd bothered to stand up and lean forward a bit. Graph-paper he already knew from his interview with Copeland who had mentioned a Mr Grant-hyphen-something or other, was Copeland's deputy. Beastly looked as if he might be next in the chain of command.

(Waterhouse, 1978: 5)

Waterhouse continues his tour of the office and in so doing reminds us of the human frailties and vanities that shape so many of our routines:

Copeland . . . waved an arm towards the dumpy office girl, a recent school-leaver by the look of her. . . . Gryce gave her a brief smile and permitted his glance, as it swivelled back to Copeland, to take a short detour via the other two females present.

Mrs Rashman must have been about fifty, ten years older than himself. That didn't necessarily rule her out. Some of these homely-looking ones really knew how to let their hair down once they'd watered the pot plants and left the office for the day, so it was rumoured. But the younger one – thirtyish? Thirty-fiveish – was probably the likelier of the two, so long as her real name proved to be something less provocative than Miss Divorce. That was definitely the once-over she had given him when the commissionaire had shown him in.

(Waterhouse, 1978: 5)

The workplace in common with most cultures, of course, builds and sustains itself around agreed routines and core beliefs. Some of these are local and distinctive, but many are time-honoured and so appear across a range of locales. Discussing refreshment in this context, Waterhouse (1978: 7–8) provides an account of an interaction that is, unlike office coffee, really worth savouring.

'Do you prefer coffee-coloured dishwater or tea-flavoured dishwater?'
    The familiar office joke made Gryce feel quite at home. 'Coffee-flavoured, I usually have'. He smiled again at the overweight junior who, with a good deal of clattering, was extracting a number of beakers from a filing cabinet and arranging them in a wire tray.
    'Don't worry we're not offending Thelma', said Seeds. 'She doesn't brew it herself, it's all untouched by 'uman 'ands'.
    'Ah, an infernal machine'.
    'The wonders of modern technology. If you press the button marked tea it pours forth a liquid resembling coffee.'
    '[W]hereas the button marked coffee produces a frothy substance that could be mistaken for tea, yes' completed Gryce.

Gryce has, thus far, been successful in his attempts to ingratiate himself with his colleague, Seeds, but there is still some work to be done associated with the routine of refreshment:

'He took a tentative sip of coffee and seeing that Seeds was looking at him in anticipation of a humorous reaction he thought of making the standard grimace of disgust, but decided instead upon raising his eyebrows and cocking his head slightly, at the same time arranging his mouth in the judicious pout of one who is prepared to concede a point in an argument'
    'I've tasted worse. I don't know when, mark you, but I have definitely tasted worse'
    'Wait till you try what passes for tea', said Seeds.
    'Oh I thought this *was* tea!'. That should have been the end of the litany but Seeds seemed to expect more, so he added: 'It's certainly an improvement on the witches' brew they used to dispense at my last billet'.

(Waterhouse, 1978: 8–9)

We could, of course, continue in this vein for quite some time. We could, as Lewis (1992) does, for example, offer a literary tour of bosses, secretarial work, boredom, and the parties that relieve this. Indeed, we could pause to consider dreams of escape and nightmares of removal. But you are I am sure, familiar with all of this . . . and more. And in any case, my intention is not to produce an exhaustive list of what Deal and Kennedy (1982) choose to ignore. Instead my intention is simply a) to remind you of what accounts of 'organizational culture' obscure and in so doing b) to illustrate the manner in which novelists such as, for example Lewis ([1922] 1994), Nobbs (1975), and Lodge (2011), and of course Waterhouse (1978) acknowledge and explore the prosaic realities of working so that we c) might develop a more faithful appreciation of the manner in which *things get done around here.*

Before we move on, however, it is worth making the point that we need not confine our 'review' to accounts of 'the workplace' as this is commonly imagined. In their accounts of the First World War, for example, Graves (2000) and Manning (2014) offer useful contrasts between 'war' and the daily routines and travails of 'soldiering' which are, in so many ways, worth reading in this context.

Yet not all routines are fully reported or indeed reportable. There is much in our daily lives that profanes the busy, serious world of those charged with leadership and change. In our next section, we will consider just some of those ways in which the public transcript (Scott, 1987) is subject to, let's say, local forms of translation and adaptation, which, while they are certainly not unknown to us, simply do not feature in accounts of culture and change.

Profanity

In this section, I will spend just a little time on what I will term the profane aspects of social organization. Readers may suggest that we have already touched upon this as we follow Gryce and his leering gaze across the office. And that is probably a fair point. Nonetheless in this section, we will acknowledge the ways in which organization (without the definite article) denies and yet enables conduct unbecoming. In this section, I will call upon the accounts of life in the Square Mile offered by Thompson (2010), Anderson (2009), and Knowles (2015).

Readers may protest that these are not novels, being instead documentary accounts of life within London's financial services industry. I accept that these texts are indeed offered to the reader as insider accounts and as documentaries of 'the city', but I cannot accept that this makes them 'reports' rather than 'stories'.

Reflecting upon his own ethnographic accounts of the workplace, Watson confesses that his academic 'reports' are in some sense creative works. Indeed, Watson (2000) tells us that his reports bear all the hallmarks of fiction because, while they offer accounts of events that were directly observed, his texts (in keeping with Gabriel's 'F' factors) render and/or rearrange these events to serve a purpose beyond that of the simple chronicler.

This is a point addressed perhaps more succinctly by Sillitoe (1979: 9). Shaking us from our lazy categorizations, he tells us that 'everything written is fiction, even non-fiction – which may be the greatest fictional non-fiction of all. . . . Anything which is not scientific or mathematical fact is coloured by the human imagination and feeble opinion'. Warming to his theme, Sillitoe adds that 'fiction' which, of course, envelopes texts that proclaim their literal truthfulness 'is a pattern of realities brought to life by suitably applied lies, and one has to be careful, in handling the laws of fiction, not to get so close to the truth that what is written loses its air of reality' (9).

Yet, while making a case for the inclusion of these profane accounts of city life within a category which I suggested would be reserved for the novelist, I will concede that I do not much like these texts. Indeed, I will observe that I actively dislike those accounts of 'city life' and high finance that have been written by men. The bile that rises in my throat as I read the accounts offered by (Lewis, 2006) and by Belfort (2007) is, I suggest, consequent upon the smugness that oozes from these texts. These individuals are, to my eyes, altogether too self-satisfied – altogether too comfortable with their own success and the boorish antics that enabled this. Those accounts of city life, penned by women, however, demonstrate perhaps a little more reflexivity insofar as the authors at least a) recognize their objectification and b) rail against the position ascribed to them as 'ladettes'[1] or surrogate office wives. Furthermore, it is worth observing that in the accounts selected here the female authors tend to experience outcomes quite unlike those visited upon their male counterparts. Lewis (2011), for example, retires and restyles himself as a functioning human and city sage, whereas women in this context continue to be assaulted and debased by forms of conduct (and excess), which the accounts offered by men such as Anderson (2009) suggest are jolly good fun. But to understand my discontents, we must be prepared to let Anderson tell us of his life as a 'Cityboy'.

Cityboys

Have you ever paused to ponder why your money-purchase pension is tanking or why the endowment policy that you purchased in the 1980s simply failed to pay off your mortgage? Anderson (2009) may have an answer for you. But you should not expect an apology.

Cityboy begins on a Sunday afternoon, on the eve of one of those periodic bank holidays that in Britain allow workers to extend their weekends.
Anderson is engaged in revels not suited to a normal Sunday evening, but
this is, in his mind, at least the eve of a bank holiday so we may wish to
cut him a little slack. Until that is, we learn that Anderson has confused his
dates. Too late, he understands that his revels are taking place on 'a school
night' and will cost us, you and me (not him), a fortune.

> With hindsight it was that fifth glass of absinthe that cost my bank £1.2
> million. A few Sunday evening pints of Old Thumper at the Masons had
> somehow graduated into the old-school booze-up a twenty-nine-year-
> old stockbroker should know better than to indulge in. While still at the
> pub some comedian had called up The Dealer and a couple of grams of
> Bolivia's finest had arrived by scooter. As I took my turn to trundle into
> the cubicle and press the crisp rolled twenty into my hungry nostrils I
> thanked God that the next day was a bank holiday Monday
>
> (Anderson, 2009: 1).

Anderson's tale is, at one level, a 'voyage and return' story, albeit one that,
for me, fails in its fifth movement. Accounting for his voyage and descent,
Anderson tells us, from the comfortable safety of a beach in Goa, that there
was, before his life as a 'Cityboy', a point in time, when having received
a religious upbringing and a degree in History from Cambridge, he wore a
pony-tail and was a functioning human being. He then tells us at length and,
with some relish, about the circumstances that caused him to succumb to the
dark forces and temptations that, it seems, await the cityboy.

To be fair, Anderson does pause now and again to suggest that throughout
this descent into the netherworld of 'the city', he was sometimes uncomfort-
able. The lighting at the sex shows, for example, seems to unsettle his aesthetic sensibilities. Although it is probably worth pointing out that he seems
little concerned as to whether the 'crack head' who is the co-respondent in
one notable sex show is actually fully capable of offering her consent!

Attending an orgy with a woman, and without the knowledge of his girl-
friend, Anderson tells us, proved to be somewhat troubling:

> 'I hadn't really thought about the fact that I'd certainly be watching my
> mistress get porked by a bunch of sweaty, swarthy Continentals'
>
> (Anderson, 2009: 318).

Despite this categorization of 'sweaty, swarthy Continentals', Anderson also
wants us to understand that he retained some (un-voiced) concerns about
what amounted to the institutionally racist hiring policy of his employer.

Looking back on his time in 'the city', Anderson concludes his 'kiss and tell' reflections of excess on a note of contrition. He wants us to understand that he is sorry for his role in the madness of the city and for the destruction wrought in the mortgage market . . . but not enough to return the cash. So if this is a 'voyage and return' tale, it is a very modern variant for while Anderson is returned to the light and to his previous hippy incarnation, he is not, properly-speaking, reunited with his community because, while he suns himself, the rest of us must continue to pay for his errors and for the Collateral Debt Obligations (CDOs) that he sold to us.

I am projecting of course. And why not? CDOs caused rather a lot of collateral damage. Yet, the fact that I really do despise Anderson and his ilk should not be allowed to obscure the realization that his account, however smug, does offer us an insight into the organized profanity that underpins the 'tough guy, macho culture' and 'the work hard/play hard' worlds of 'the city'.

But what is it like to be a woman in this set-up? What is it like to be 'the other' in a cultural context that worships at the temple Dionysus? Knowles (2015) and Thompson (2010) offer some insights.

Not cityboys

Booker reminds us that stories often turn upon perspective: David's success is after all Goliath's tragic downfall. The account of city life developed by Knowles (2015) offers, I suggest, a very clear example of the operation of this law of perspective.

Knowles (2015), it would be fair to suggest, was from but was not of the 'tough guy, macho culture' of 'the city'. She was, as we shall see, subject to but not properly a part of this culture because, as Personal Assistant (PA), her role was to support those prepared to take monstrous risks with the money of others.

Knowles reminds us what 'support' means in this context. Like so many PAs, she was expected to subordinate her needs and identity to the needs of her boss. She was, for example, expected to shop on his behalf, to arrange his dental appointments, chase his surveyors, file his medical reports, and to arrange his birthday celebrations. Beyond these routine indignities, however, Knowles was, she tells us, obliged to navigate a cultural formation notable for leering, drug-taking, extramarital affairs, the open display of pornography, and (semi) public displays of masturbation.

The text developed by Knowles, perhaps unsurprisingly, concludes in much the same way as Anderson's insofar as she, too, proclaims that life is just too short to remain long in this sort of setting. But where Anderson's journey represents an escape from excess and addiction, Knowles's (2015:

296) passage represents a return from the brink of a nervous breakdown – a reprieve from constantly 'feeling oppressed or scared'. Deprived of wealth, unlike Anderson, Knowles reports not from the beach but from another office where a more helpful boss offers her support and in so doing provides consolation within a context populated *only* by the everyday 'weirdos', which would have been familiar to Waterhouse.

But at least Knowles gets to choose the manner of her exit. Thompson (2010), as we shall see, was not afforded this opportunity.

Thompson (2010: 14), one of the few female inter-dealer bond brokers active in 'the city', it seems, embraced (pretty) much all of the vices that the 'dark power' made available to Anderson. Her narrative begins as follows:

> My alarm sounded, providing a cheerful calypso soundtrack to accompany the beams of blue light emanating from the muted television set. It was 5.45 a.m., Thursday morning. January 2007. I was lying seminaked on the floor beside my bed, a half-eaten matzo perched atop my right breast, my Chanel handbag lying faithfully at my feet, its contents strewn across the floor. I rolled slowly onto my side and hit snooze on my Blackberry, waiting for the familiar pounding above my left temple and the waves of nausea to begin, as the cracker crumbled into the stained beige carpet beneath me.

Yet having had the temerity to publish an article which reveals what every insider knows to be a faithful account of 'the city' and its debasement, Thompson is summarily dismissed for gross misconduct.

I will confess that I have little real sympathy for Thompson: Even a loose reading of HR policy suggests that her conduct was, while pretty much normal, highly inappropriate. But this should not prevent us from acknowledging a) the profane reality of her workplace and b) the manner in which commentators on organizational culture and change have resolutely refused to address its countenance.

If there was ever a culture in need of change, it is surely that of 'the city'!

In our next section, we will consider the polyphony denied by those who protest that organizational culture is a monological monolith which determines our conduct.

Polyphony

To explore organizational polyphony, I will consider Jeff Torrington's (1996) *The Devil's Carousel*. This text, loosely based upon Torrington's working life within the Rootes/Chrsyler factory based at Linwood in Scotland, offers a number of related short stories built around the 'Centaur Car

Company' and its production line. I have selected this text because in following the lives and private travails of those employed by this car company, Torrington produces a multi-voiced account of a culture that assaults our senses and our sensibilities.

Torrington's characters are, I suggest, almost Dobuan in their habits and manners. They are suspicious and mutually mistrustful almost to the point of paranoia. Indeed, as far as the rank-and-file employees of the Centaur Car Company are concerned, 'Management' is so removed for the realities of the production line and so hostile to normal human concerns and reciprocities that they are 'Martians'.

Between each of the chapters that constitute the book, further critical information on the Martians is offered by 'the Laffing Anarkist' – a publication that exists to challenge and to lampoon the company.

The universe jointly constructed by Torrington and his 'laffing anarkist', we should note, covers a range of the basic plots considered by Booker (2007). The 10 short stories offered include, for example

- a head of security who on his retirement is presented with a pair of binoculars which, when he looks through them for the first time, finally allow him to see the gang of thieves who have evaded him;
- a religious evangelist who demands that his subordinates remove the pornography that decorates their work space only to find that images of his own daughter are among those displayed; and
- a man employed on permanent night shift who learns just why it is that his wife insists on this pattern of work.

Together these tales and more offer a pretty profane account of work and working. The world defined by *The Devil's Carousel* is, we should note, plainly a noisy, seedy, and grubby one. But beyond this profanity, Torrington successfully produces a multi-voiced account of the workplace. Crucially, *The Devil's Carousel* opens to us a world where macho men refuse to be bullied by 'the Martians'; where 'non-work' fills the day; where failed plans, hurt, loss, damage, and theft are simply a part of the routine . . . albeit that part missed by the likes of Deal and Kennedy.

This is not to suggest, of course, that the polyphony developed by Torrington is in any sense complete or even wholesome. The Centaur Car Company is, after all, largely populated by men, and it is largely a man's world (with fragile egos, macho posturing, and cheap pornography) that Torrington creates. Yet, the point remains that in *The Devil's Carousel*, the social organization of the Centaur Car Company is revealed to us as complex, porous, and unlike so many representations of culture (and change), fragmented and multi-voiced.

Gabriel (2000), of course, insists that all poetic tales are, in contrast to 'reports' essentially polyphonic. And this is undoubtedly true. Yet, Torrington's text is instructive. Here, the polyphony is so loud that the noise becomes, I suggest, the signal!

In our final thread, we will respond to this signal. I will therefore offer brief reflections designed to summarize and to lash together the arguments developed throughout this little book.

Note

1 This grisly term emerged in the 1990s and was used to refer to a group of women whom, it was asserted, engaged routinely in hard-drinking and casual sex. Noting that such conduct was more typically associated with young men, it was suggested that these women had transgressed gender boundaries and had become 'ladettes'.

7   Concluding comments

This little book has been designed to rethink organizational culture. It has, consequently, offered a critical appreciation and review of organizational culture. In pursuit of this review, we have placed the study of organizational culture within an historical frame that can trace and account for the manner in which the study of how people think, feel, act, and indeed interact at work has been constituted. Noting that notions of 'culture' have been imported from academic sociology, we have considered the constitution of social action within this domain. Indeed, we have observed that 'culture', within the American academy, was constituted as a residual matter, subordinate to, and, peculiarly, separated from social action. Commenting upon this approach and upon the outcomes that it promotes, Kuper (1999) argues, that the pioneering American academics developed descriptively rich but under-theorized accounts of culture that amount to little more than inventories of artefacts.

Reflecting upon the British School, Kuper acknowledges the revolution in fieldwork led by Malinowski, which encouraged social anthropologists to construct the world from the perspective of 'the native'. Nonetheless, he laments the inability of Malinowski's functionalism to accommodate and to account for the everyday social dynamics that cause and allow cultural change.

Turning our attention to the study of organizational or workplace cultures, we have argued that, while the 'cultural turn' plainly accelerated in the 1980s and became a central concern for practitioners and for academics in this period, earlier scholars had, plainly, recognized that social organization might usefully be constituted in cultural terms.

Focusing upon the accounts developed throughout the 1980s, we have argued that these remain pre-Malinowskian inasmuch as they offer:

a)   inventories of artefacts, rather than theoretically mature analyses and
b)   top-down views of culture which
c)   derive their understanding of culture from the experiences of a small, and privileged, elite.

Reflecting upon the manner in which this pre-Malinowskian approach has acted to inform and yet deform our appreciation of culture, we have analysed the typologies offered by Deal and Kennedy (1982), Handy ([1978] 2010, 1985), Schein (1985), and Hofstede (1980, 1991; Hofstede, Hofstede and Minkov, 2010). I have argued that these frameworks distort appreciation of the social dynamics of the workplace and now, some 40 years on from their original publication, should be treated as cultural artefacts – expressions of privilege that must now be challenged. To secure this review and reconsideration, we have argued that the models outlined in this book (and indeed in pretty much all of the textbooks developed for students) might now be set aside in favour of a pedagogy that speaks to the whole classroom and the community beyond.

In an attempt to develop an account of organization that can reveal and account for the privilege expressed in and through models of organizational culture, we have argued that steps should be taken, now, to reconstitute our understanding of the norms, values, and beliefs that shape social organization. We have, therefore, argued for an account of organizations-as-cultures understood as pluralities from the bottom-up.

Following Wright-Mills (1973), I have suggested that students and scholars of organization might embark upon this new pedagogy a) by reading novels and b) by engaging in more conventional forms of research designed to seek out the voices and perspectives, excluded from the analytical frame.

To this end and to encourage reflection on the realities of working and organizing, I have offered texts and tales that index polyphony, profanity, and the organizationally prosaic. These tales of profanity of the prosaic and of polyphony are useful, I suggest, because they address the persistent anxieties, problems, and routines that arise in and through organizations. In addition, these tales reflect our intuition as to the complexity of social organization and, so, offer to those inclined to listen, a useful appreciation of *how things get done around here.*

Bibliography

Ackroyd, S and Crowdy, PA (1990) 'Can culture be managed? Working with raw material: The case of the English slaughtermen', *Personnel Review*, 19 (5): 3–13.

Anderson, G (2009) *Cityboy: Beer and Loathing in the Square Mile*, Headline Books: London.

Aristotle (1965) *The Politics*, trans. TS Dorsch, Penguin: London.

Atkinson, P (1997) *Creating Culture Change: Strategies for Success*, Rushmere Wynne: London.

Belfort, J (2007) *The Wolf of Wall Street: How Money Destroyed a Wall Street Superman*, Bantam Books: New York, NY.

Benedict, R [1934] (1989) *Patterns of Culture*, Houghton Mifflin Company: Boston, MA.

Booker, C (2007) *The Seven Basic Plots: Why We Tell Stories*, Continuum: London.

Braverman, H (1974) *Labor and Monopoly Capital*, Free Press: New York, NY.

Brown, A (1995) *Organisational Culture*, Pitman: London.

Buchanan, D and Huczynski, A (1997) *Organizational Behaviour*, Cassell: London.

Burrell, G (1997) *Pandemonium*, Sage: London.

Burrell, G and Morgan, G (1979) *Sociological Paradigms and Organizational Analysis*, Heinemann: London.

Butterfield, H [1931] (1973) *The Whig Interpretation of History*, Pelican Books: Harmondsworth, Middlesex.

Collins, D (1998) *Organizational Change: Sociological Perspectives*, Routledge: London and New York.

Collins, D (2000) *Management Fads and Buzzwords: Critical-Practical Perspectives*, Routledge: London and New York.

Collins, D (2007) *Narrating the Management Guru: In Search of Tom Peters*, Taylor and Francis, Routledge: London and New York.

Collins, D (2012) 'Women roar: The "women's thing" in the storywork of Tom Peters', *Organization*, 19 (4): 405–424.

Collins, D (2013) 'In search of popular management: Sensemaking, sensegiving and storytelling in the excellence project', *Culture and Organization*, 19 (1): 42–61.

Collins, D (2018) *Stories for Management Success: The Power of Talk in Organizations*, Taylor and Francis, Routledge: Abingdon, Oxon and New York.

Collins, D (2021a) *Management Gurus: A Research Overview*, Taylor and Francis, Routledge: Abingdon, Oxon and New York.

Collins, D (2021b) *The Organizational Storytelling Workbook: How to Harness This Powerful Management and Communication Tool*, Taylor and Francis, Routledge: Abingdon, Oxon and New York.

Collins, D and Rainwater, K (2005) 'Managing change at sears: A sideways look at a celebrated tale of corporate transformation', *Journal of Organizational Change Management*, 18 (1): 16–30.

Crainer, S (1997) *Corporate Man to Corporate Skunk: The Tom Peters Phenomenon: A Biography*, Capstone: Oxford.

Deal, TE and Kennedy, AA (1982) *Corporate Cultures*, Penguin: Harmondsworth.

Deal, TE and Kennedy, AA (1999) *The New Corporate Cultures: Revitalizing the Workplace after Downsizing, Mergers and Reengineering*, Orion Business Books: London.

Dickens, C [1841] (1922) *A Christmas Carol*, Cecil Palmer: London.

Feldman, SP (1986) 'Management in context: An essay on the relevance of culture to the understanding of organizational change', *Journal of Management Studies*, 23 (6): 587–607.

Freeman, R and Medoff, JL (1984) *What Do Unions Do?* Basic Books: New York, NY.

Gabriel, Y (2000) *Storytelling in Organizations: Facts, Fictions and Fantasies*, Oxford University Press: Oxford.

Gabriel, Y (2004) 'Narratives, Stories and Texts' in Grant D, Hardy, C and Oswick, C (eds), *The Sage Handbook of Organizational Discourse*, Sage: London.

Geneen, H and Moscow, A (1986) *Managing*, Grafton Books: London.

Graves, R (2000) *Goodbye to All That*, Penguin: Harmondsworth, Middlesex.

Hall, ET (1976) *Beyond Culture: Essays on Literature and Learning*, Anchor Books: London.

Handy, C [1978] (2010) *The Gods of Management*, Penguin: London.

Handy, C (1985) *Understanding Organizations*, Penguin: London.

Harrison, R (1972) 'How to describe your organization', *Harvard Business Review*, 50 (May/June): 119–128.

Hofstede, G (1980) *Cultures' Consequences: International Differences in Work-Related Values*, Sage: Thousand Oaks, CA.

Hofstede, G (1991) *Cultures and Organizations: Software of the Mind*, McGraw-Hill: London.

Hofstede, G, Hofstede, GJ and Minkov, M (2010) *Cultures and Organizations: Software of the Mind*, 3rd edn, McGraw-Hill: London.

Independent 25/08/2020 'Boris Johnson says time to stop "cringing embarrassment" about British history after BBC Proms drop Rule Britannia lyrics'.

Jaques, E (1951) *The Changing Culture of a Factory: A Study of Authority and Participation in an Industrial Setting*, Tavistock: London.

Kanter, RM (1989) *When Giants Learn to Dance*, Simon and Schuster: London.

Knowles, VA (2015) *The PA's Story: Sex, Salaries and Square Mile Sleaze*, John Blake Publishing: London.

Kuehling, S (2005) *Dobu: Ethics of Exchange on a Massim Island, Papua New Guinea*, Hawaii University Press: Honolulu.

Kuper, A (1996) *Anthropology and Anthropologists: The Modern British School*, 2nd edn, Routledge: London.

Kuper, A (1999) *Culture: The Anthropologist's View*, Harvard: Cambridge, MA.

Latour, B (1987) *Science in Action*, Harvard University Press: Cambridge, MA.

Lewis, J (1992) *The Chatto Book of Office Life or Love among the Filing Cabinets*, Chatto and Windus: London.

Lewis, M (2006) *Liar's Poker*, Hodder Paperbacks: London.

Lewis, M (2011) *The Big Short: Inside the Doomsday Machine*, Penguin: Harmondsworth, Middlesex.

Lewis, S [1922] (1994) *Babbit*, Vintage Classics: New York, NY.

Lodge, D (2011) *Nice Work*, Secker and Warburg: London.

Lutz, B (2011) *Car Guys versus Bean Counters: The Battle for the Soul of American Business*, Portfolio and Penguin: New York, NY.

Macur, J (2014) *Cycle of Lies: The Fall of Lance Armstrong*, William Collins: London.

Manning, F (2014) *The Middle Parts of Fortune: Somme and Ancre, 1916*, Penguin: Harmondsworth, Middlesex.

Mars, G (1982) *Cheats at Work: An Anthropology of Workplace Crime*, Unwin Paperbacks: London.

Martin, J (1992) *Cultures in Organizations: Three Perspectives*, Oxford University Press: Oxford.

Martin, J, Feldman, MS, Hatch, MJ and Sitkin, SB (1983) 'The uniqueness paradox in organizational stories', *Administrative Science Quarterly*, 28: 438–453.

McCrone, D (1993) *Understanding Scotland: The Sociology of a Stateless Nation*, Routledge: London.

McSweeney, B (2002) 'Hofstede's model of national cultural differences and their consequences: A triumph of faith: A failure of analysis', *Human Relations*, 55: 89–118.

Mintzberg, H (1973) *The Nature of Managerial Work*, Harper and Row: New York.

Nobbs, D (1975) *The Death of Reginald Perrin*, Penguin: Harmondsworth, Middlesex.

Ogbonna, E and Wilkinson, B (1988) 'Corporate strategy and corporate culture: The management of change in the UK supermarket industry', *Personnel Review*, 7 (6): 10–14.

Parker, T (1993) *May the Lord in His Mercy Be Kind to Belfast*, Jonathan Cape: London.

Pascale, RT and Athos, AG [1981] (1986) *The Art of Japanese Management*, Sidgwick and Jackson: London.

Peters, T and Waterman, R (1982) *In Search of Excellence*, Harper and Row: New York.

Schein, E (1985) *Organizational Culture and Leadership*, Jossey-Bass: San Francisco.

Scott, JC (1987) *Weapons of the Weak: Everyday Forms of Peasant Resistance*, Yale University Press: New Haven, CT.

Sellar, WC and Yeatman, RJ [1930] (1938) *1066 and All That: A Memorable History of England, Comprising All the Parts That You Can Remember, Including 103 Good Things, 5 Bad Kings and 2 Genuine Dates*, Methuen and Co: London.

Sillitoe, A (1979) *Raw Material*, W H Allen and Co: London.

Sims, D, Fineman, S and Gabriel, Y (1993) *Organizing and Organizations*, Sage: London.

Taylor, FW (1911) *The Principles of Scientific Management*, Harper and Row: New York.

Thompson, P and McHugh, D (1990) *Work Organizations: A Critical Introduction*, Palgrave MacMillan: Basingstoke.

Thompson, V (2010) *Gross Misconduct: My Year of Excess in the City*, Pocket Books: London.

Torrington, J (1996) *The Devil's Carousel*, Secker and Warburg: London.

Walsh, D (2013) *Seven Deadly Sins: My Pursuit of Lance Armstrong*, Simon and Schuster: London.

Waterhouse, K (1978) *Office Life: A Novel*, Michael Joseph: London.

Watson, T (2000) 'Ethnographic fiction science: Making sense of managerial work and organizational research processes with Caroline and Terry', *Organization*, 7: 489–510.

Weick, K (1995) *Sensemaking in Organizations*, Sage: London.

Weisberger, L (2003) *The Devil Wears Prada*, Harper Collins: London.

Whyte, WH [1956] (1961) *The Organization Man*, Penguin: Harmondsworth.

Wright, S (1994) *Anthropology of Organizations*, Routledge: London.

Wright-Mills, C (1973) *The Sociological Imagination*, Penguin: Harmondsworth.

Index

Note: Page numbers in *italics* indicate a figure on the corresponding page.

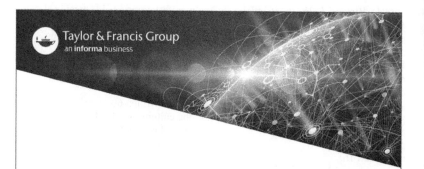